Being With Horses
By Nahshon Cook

Foreword

I first encountered Nahshon's work at the Rocky Mountain Horse Expo in the spring of 2019. I was busy that weekend managing multiple demonstrations and found myself running around the expo center at a dizzying pace—but when I heard Nahshon's voice over the loudspeaker, something stopped me in my tracks.

It wasn't just what I heard him saying, it was how he was saying it. His voice radiated groundedness, centeredness, presence, compassion, and wisdom in a way that was absolutely magnetic. It pulled me from my rushing about and into the arena, where I sat in awe for the duration of his presentation. I watched the transformation taking place in that arena that day—both in the horses and their riders—and was immediately a fan of Nahshon's.

When he told me of his plans for writing a book, I couldn't have been more ecstatic. His voice deserves to be heard, and we owe it to our horses to listen.

After teaching hundreds of students around the globe how to connect with their horses, I've become aware of common blocks to connection that keep people at war with their horses and eventually cause them to give up on their lifelong dream of building a relationship with these animals altogether. Through his profound wisdom, Nahshon offers balm to these wounds that keep us from connecting and teaches us how to build a container where magic can happen between species.

Nahshon teaches us how to listen to our horses in every moment, thereby prioritizing our horses' emotions and opening the lines for conversation and connection. Whenever we make a request to our horse, she responds with how she feels about that request. The majority of people miss the subtle ways she tries to talk to us and hence miss an opportunity for us to understand and connect more deeply with her.

When her whispers are ignored and dismissed, she grows louder in her attempts to be heard and resorts to survival instincts of fight, flight, or freeze. In the past, this has led to a history of silencing the horse's voice, as humans attempted to overpower her and force her into compliance.

Nahshon lays the path towards connection instead of compliance by teaching us how to open our eyes, ears, and hearts to what she is saying—and it is about time she is heard.

But Nahshon doesn't just teach you about more ethical and compassionate methods of connecting with the horse on a mental, physical, emotional and spiritual level—he teaches us how to build a new relationship to life, opening our eyes to how we can restore harmony and balance not only with our horses, but with ourselves, other humans and our planet.

It has been said that the horse is a mirror to your soul. Nahshon teaches us how to look into that mirror and learn and grow from the reflections our horses reveal to us. He also teaches us how to tune into the frequency of connection in ways that may surprise you because they go against the way many of us have been conditioned to think and behave.

• In a world where we prioritize the outcome, goal, and end result, Nahshon teaches us surrender to the process and find presence in each step we take.

• In a world where we prioritize analyzing, logic, and thinking, Nahshon teaches us to drop out of our minds and into our hearts and bodies to feel.

• In a world where we prioritize conquering, controlling and forcing, Nahshon teaches us to soften and co-create with our horse. Training becomes something we do with the horse not to her.

• In a world where we prioritize human intelligence and dominion, Nahshon teaches us how to trust in and be led by the wisdom of the horse.

The spirit of the horse is speaking through Nahshon. I am so grateful for who he is and for the medicine that he is sharing with the world.

Mustang Maddy (Madison Shambaugh)
May 2021

Author's Note

Dear Reader,

Hello! It was suggested, since many of you don't know me from a dew drop, that I write a letter of introduction about who I am, what the inspiration for **Being With Horses** was, and what I hope you get from reading it. So, here we go:

1) My name is Nahshon Cook. I'm a horseman, a poet, and an essayist. I help the broken gift-horses piece themselves back together again. Those wounded-soul ones who are only able to accept your help to the extent that you're willing to allow them to show you yourself.

2) The broken gift-horses are a huge education that has brought me to demoralizingly humbled tears of surrender, and gratitude, and joy many times. Helping them heal is teaching me how to love myself better, and other people, too; and that healthy relationships, whomever with, are well-gardened flower beds.

3) Thank you for reading this note, Dear Reader, and I hope, with my whole heart, that you enjoy the rest of the journey that **Being With Horses** is.

Love,
Nahshon

#0

Those who master
being with horses
master being with horses
because they love others.
Love is the medicine.

#1

There's been more than one occasion
that I've tried to stop training horses

because people scared me:
I didn't know how to effectively

communicate with people.
I'm most at home in my heart

when I'm with horses, because,
for me, horses are heaven. But,

horses come with people, and so
I had to learn to love people, too. ⸺ *Just Like*
Veterinarians

#2

1)

One: you're safe. Two: this lesson is not a performance. Three: there's no judgement. I'm just here to try and help and I hope that I can. Ok? So, let's just see what we've got and let me know when you're ready for me to jump in.

2)

What a beautiful little horse. She goes, "Who you callin' little. I'm not little." But, she holds on to everything. She takes everything personally. She's kind of set up a cage for herself, though. She doesn't know how to get out of it. My mare, Mohawk, is like that.

3)

So, what I'd like you to do first is just breathe. You're not breathing in your body. Don't let what you think are your imperfections fuck everything up. Just breathe and we'll start where we're at. Walk your mare around. Feel your feet on the floor.

release self judgements

4)

What I'd like you to do is go through the places in your body where you're tense, and put your mind there, and guide the breath there, and try and open those spaces with the breath. Don't try to force the tension away. Be gentle, like a dew drop.

5)

The hardest thing to do with ourselves is be kind.

6)

Let your belly out, just relax. Breathe deep, deep down into your body. Try and spread your toes out in your boots, relax the backs of your knees. It opens up the hips, did you feel that? Very good. Now you can slowly feed her line out, and keep walking with her. And just offer, don't expect. And if she wants to stay with you, she'll stay with you. If she's ready to make the circle a little bigger, she will.

7)

Make sure that you relax your butt-cheeks. There! Now she's starting to let go. Very good. Tops of your shoulders at the base of your neck, breathe into that space. And as it relaxes, you'll begin to feel it all the way back down through the scapula. Look, she's starting to chew!

8)

Do you feel how your knees are starting to move a little better because your feet aren't locked? I know that because horses lock at the base of their necks when we're locked in our hip flexors. And usually our hip flexors are locked because our toes are cramped, and it tenses our quadriceps, which is usually why we hunch over. When we open our feet, it releases the tendons behind the backs of our knees, and the muscle chain unlocks, and there are our hip flexors, and then there's our stomach, and our lower back. Feel that? Good.

9)
If you trust the breath it'll get you through life.

10)
Now your mare is softening, because you're softening. Very Good. Now, what I'd like you to do is imagine the warmth coming down through your hand to her rein, and just breathe into the rein. That's it, her throat is starting to open up. Good. Trust her.

11)
What are you feeling?

12)
Breathe into the place where there's tension. Breathe into your back. Breathe into the part of your back that you're protecting. Good, you just stood up straighter, and you're not looking at the floor. Breathe into your back. There. What emotion are you finding in that space where you're protecting your back?

explore The need to Self Protect. - Survival instincts Why?

5

13)

Feel it, and let it go. Stay with that space. Now she's softening. Hallelujah!

14)

Now, the importance of what you've just found is beginning to understand when you started believing that you weren't enough, and more importantly, where and, from whom, you learned that. You can give voice to it, or not. But, what I want you to do is have the courage to allow the space to go away. ~ over + over again

15)

As you start to let that stuff move, you may feel a little tension in the tailbone. Breathe into that space. Yeah. It's okay. It's okay. It's okay. Breathe into it. Don't stop the tears. Do you feel how your steps have now started to relax? Very good.

16)

Now I know she's opening up because she's aware of the world, but she's focused on you. That's what you want. We're not looking for obedience, first. We're looking for trust.

17)

Good. Now, as you continue to breathe, put the tongue to the roof of your mouth and it'll relax the muscles in your face, and breathe in-and-out of your nose if you can do so safely with your mask on. You'll start to feel your ears open up, and the stiffness in the back of your neck begins to go away.

Do you feel that? Yes? Very good. And the beautiful thing is, is that as we're going through the process of these considerations, you're standing up straighter; you're not guarding your heart anymore. Consequently, neither is she. She's following your lead.

18)
Very good. Now the lesson can begin.

#3

Today, I received a question from a kiddo who asked when my passion for horses started.

I told her, *Last lifetime I think. It's always been there.*

I told her, *I've done a lot with horses and have decided that the most important thing I can do*
          as a trainer and a teacher is help them feel happy by giving them a place to be safe.

I told her, *I've learned that if I do that, they'll do anything for me.*

#4

People being kind to themselves isn't forgiveness in the form of a religious merit-making giving of alms. But rather, as a practice of letting go of regret to create space for the possibility of new feelings to come in. One of the biggest motivations for people to work with horses as an art, in the form of feel, is usually born out of guilt over how we've seen horses treated in the past. Horses don't do well with our guilt, and I'm really grateful for that.

For me, the value in the undertaking of horses helping people learn to live feelingly is that they teach us that searching elsewhere for our answers means looking in the mirror, and having the courage to allow what we understand to come from a place of insight instead of mimicry. Now, the challenge of our work with horses is understanding that they don't have watches or calendars. The time that health-giving work takes is what it is, like nature nurturing ideas, customs, and the social behaviors of a society that are deeply rooted in love so that we can all heal and be healed because we are each other's gifts of grace.

Now, to allow ourselves to be available to the energy that connects humans to horses so that partnership is possible, we have to be mindful of how they feel when we're approaching them, and how we feel when they're approaching us.

It's a reciprocity built on body language, and subtlety, and emotional response blossoming out of the silent stillness that holding space is; which means having the courage to wait.

Also, it's an important thing to understand that we can't truly make horses do what they don't want to. What reason are we giving them to make our work with them more interesting than eating grass? Better yet, how can we find a way to use a horse wanting to eat grass as a segue for our work with him or her? Motivating ourselves enough to learn how to communicate with horses in a way that allows horses to feel motivated enough to tell you what they hear us saying is what this way of being is all about. Are your questions clear enough to receive the answers you're asking the horses for? If not, it's probably because you're waiting for the horse to respond instead of react. Responding is outside of the horses's nature.

That said, a mind in good spirits is a focused mind. We make healthier progress when we're not judging ourselves through the lens of self-doubt.

Now, those horses that we have the most trouble with are the horses that usually reflect those parts of ourselves back to us that we don't want to see. So then the question becomes, "What fear are we afraid of facing?" and, more importantly, "How did we learn to be afraid of facing that fear?" It's us learning how we learned how to be afraid that will help us face the fear we're afraid to face. When a person can learn to use fear as a guide for growth, they are free.

So, just having your horse as an example: you felt guilty that you made all of your mistakes on him, and now you're afraid that because you did that to him, he doesn't want to be with you, when the real fear is of you not knowing how to be powerful enough to stay present when you're with him.

The most holy thing in this whole practice of having interests and finding meaning is relationships. That's what horses have taught me. And that even though people have been the cause of every painful experience I've ever had, people are worthy of my healthy attention, because I'm worthy of my horse's healthy attention.

My horses teachings have changed me. They've grown me out of personhood and peopleishness, and turned me into a human being. That's the most beautiful road any one person could ever travel, I think: the one that allows you to see that everything you see is just a reflection of you seeing what you see. And the deeper I go into my pain, the easier it is to understand that the people who gifted it to me did so out of their only point of reference for that particular shared space in a past relationship, which allows me to have compassion for them, which is how I stay away from bitterness. Forgiveness.

You're on the right track. It's usually those moments when it feels like everything has just fallen to shit, and that nothing is worth your time anymore, that you're the closest to finding what you're looking for. All that to say: don't stop walking. All that to say: be mindful of where you're holding tension in your body when you're with the gelding that triggers your fear response. As soon as you allow breath into that tension in your body, he will start to soften. Not by anything you're doing to him, but by everything that you're intentionally changing in yourself while you're in his realm. Does that make sense?

And this is the thing about a lifetime, as I understand it: getting to a place isn't as important as being fully aware of where you are along the way, which is connection. Connection is broken once you think there's a place you have to arrive at, because then your focus is on perfection and not progress. Doing grows out of Being. Being grows out of the ability to hold space, which is the mind realizing that each moment of the journey is a journey of its own.

Everything that allows us to practice paying attention is meditation, which simply means: do we have the courage to be still enough to start? And start again. And start again, and again, and again from a place in which our power is true, so that we can use it as an anchor to help us be strong in the places we are weak. My mom once told me, "When you stop running after what you think will make you happy, and stop running away from what you think will make you sad, you find yourself. That's a good place to be." Sometimes, to grow, we must unlearn everything we've been taught to know. So, strive gently.

#5

if we each carry
around a book
of our thoughts
and to think
is to listen
then the world
becomes like a river
where something
happening on one end
is echoed on the other
much like a horse's spine
the cervical spine to the hocks
the thoracic spine to the hips
the lumbar spine to the stifle
with this understanding
i'm able to heal
some horses
seemingly beyond repair
in body and mind
when I feel lost
and words escape me
because my heart is broken
I go to the barn
and sit with my horses

and allow them
to wrap me in their peace like a hug
the morning after
I watched George Floyd
cry out for his mother
before he breathed
his last breath
I went into Nova's stall
wanting to pray
and trying to pray
but I couldn't

#6

It's not about controlling your horse. Controlling her means you're afraid of her. And I don't know that you'll ever be out of fear, but you're learning how to handle being afraid so that it's not paralyzing you anymore. I will never forget when I was sitting in that chair, and you were standing right there holding her lead rope, and I told you to walk, and you couldn't un-freeze your feet from the floor because you where so terrified of her exploding. That was our first lesson.

Now, you feel like you have more control on the ground, lunging her, because you're not afraid of letting go of your fear of her exploding, because you have your feet, because you're separate from her. Here's my task today: to help you find the courage to not be separate from your horse.

This is what I'd like you to do: try and imagine that her hind legs are in your seat bones, and that her front legs are coming out of your hip sockets, and give your body to her movement. Good. Let the rein out a little bit more. Now, when one of your thighs is down, step down into the stirrup on that same side. Good. Step. Step. Step. Step. Good. Offer your hands by scratching her neck. Good, open up your body. Good. You feel her back lift? Good. You did that on a release of the hand. She goes, "This feels really good." You, my dear, are touching communication. Now, we can begin to learn how to ride.

The heart of healthy riding is clarity. The heart of clarity is balance. The heart of balance is relaxation. The heart of relaxation is trust. Your technique grows out of what you have trust in. Do you trust the chaos, or do you you trust the calm? Either way, your horse responds accordingly. It's all the same energy, it's just a matter of how you use it. Calm is based on you feeling in your body. Chaos is based on you emoting in your mind. When you're in your body, following her body, it's like the ocean. It's just like floating in the ocean. If you surrender, and feel, you float. If you fight, and emote, you sink. Your horse is the ocean.

Now, mind how your mind can't be any place other than the present-moment; feel when you're surrendering to the ocean. Just feel it; how it moves your body and tries to heal your heart-hurts and is freedom if you want be free. Observe how Doing grows out of Being. Being is Doing's heart. Being afraid is a learned behavior, which means it can be unlearned if you're willing to start working through your stuck-point. What is your stuck-point?

Her spooking.

So, if she spooks, what happens?

I lose control.

But, what if she doesn't spook?

I don't know.

Okay, try. Forward!

Good. Do you feel the feeling of peace you're creating in this arena? You're doing that. And because you're speaking out of that peaceful feeling, that's all she's able to hear you say: peace. That's the power you have. But, you didn't find it until control over everything other than yourself was no longer the key to your being able to grow in the ways that you want. Absolutely brilliant!

You've stretched your courage far today; and you were born into something new, and more possible for you and your horse to enjoy, instead of just being barely bearable enough for each of you to endure. And you see: the more you trusted her, the more she trusted you.

#7

Every horse should have a life.

Every horse should have a purpose.

Every horse, no matter how handicapped
can learn to do something useful
to the very best of his or her ability
if given the chance.

#8

A student I've been working with for nearly five years came to her lesson today and said, "Today, I need you to teach me how to teach" and then just wept. She'll be moving away with her family, and we won't be able to work together much anymore.

I told her no one had ever asked me to teach them how to do that before, and I'm not sure I can, but I'd try.

So I did like I always do when I'm supposed to begin, but don't know how. I started asking questions. (The way someone answers lets me know what it is they are really asking.)

I told her I'm always afraid at the beginning of my lessons because I never know what to expect, which is true. People come to me and pay me good money to help them see what they can't, and the hardest part about that is trusting the truth of the moment enough to be honest.

I told her when I try to be perfect, I forget to breathe and can't find the words I need to teach with.

I told her the challenges horses have in training are never the horse's fault, and I've not been called back to work with some people because I told them the wall they'd run into was either because their horse wasn't mentally or physically able, or it didn't understand what was being asked. But punishment to get their point across was neither warranted nor supported as a solution by me.

I told her her responsibility to people is to teach them how to feel more than how to ride. As long as she stays courageous enough to be present and open and vulnerable, the horses will show her how to help people do that. The answer to horse training challenges is always where horses are. This is a healing art.

I told her she could always call me whenever she needed, and I'd help the best I know how.

Body to light, light to world.

That was my last lesson for today—and one of the hardest ever.

#9

There was this beautiful duplet of realizations about horses waltzing around in my heart last week that, unconsciously, in my work with them, is the truth I grow daily in understanding of. But, now that they've found words I can share with, they are another tool I can use to teach, and they are:

1) Happy horses heal hurting human hearts.

2) As we strive to heal our hurting hearts by keeping our horses as happy as we can, we begin to see some things we've done for and with them that weren't so enlightened, even though it's the best we could do, for whatever reason, at the time.

3) And that self-reflection blossoming into self-criticism blossoming into forgiveness blossoming into positive change is a beautiful path along the journey to becoming our best selves for our own selves, and for our horses, and for each other.

#10

Cosmonaut came to my family's farm a few months ago shivering in sweat-drenched fear, and with a manila folder holding some of his past life story, the applicable vaccination records, and a list of things it was believed he couldn't do anymore. His behavioral needs were of such concern to the rescue that they wouldn't allow anyone to adopt him without a trainer whose way of working with horses was observed on-site and approved by staff.

Cosmonaut, a beautiful, 12-year-old, dark bay, 17 hand, Dutch Warmblood gelding lived at the rescue for two years after having been dropped off by his previous people for re-fusing to jump jumps anymore. The overdeveloped muscles under his neck, and the tension in his lower back, behind where the saddle would sit, led me to conclude that Cosmonaut had been trained and ridden in a way that over-strained his spine and hindlimb joints and put added weight on his forelimbs.

Cosmonaut had likely stopped working because the work was causing him pain, the easing of which lay in creating a correct, structurally sound top line. But, before the work on Cosmonaut's body could carry on, I had to undo the glass fortress he'd built around his mind. He was heart-hurt and had lost all hope in human hands for anything other than trials, tribulation and treats.

Cosmonaut loves treats! So, I use them as a tool to teach him behaviors I want him to learn for the simple fact that rewarded behaviors are more likely to be repeated. That said, any behavior is teachable if it is not physically impossible, and we can offer the horse new experiences in which to learn. For Cosmonaut, that new experience was target training, which has taught him to concentrate on a target I point to when I say, "Touch!" because he associates the word command with an action, which in-turn triggers vocal praise (e.g. "Good Boy!"), which guarantees a goodie!

In its infancy, my capacities as a trainer were based on the belief that my role in relationship to horses was to talk and lead. But, as my practice has matured I've begun to see my true value lives in me listening and being led. Horses only have two ways of communicating how what we're asking makes them feel: relax or evade. If the latter is the answer we're continually confronted with, then we must re-examine our methods and practices of teaching and refine them until the horse feels acknowledged enough to de-stress. With horses in training, if a safe space is in place for the process to take the time it takes, we can usually get where we're going because we're able to start where we're at.

Cosmonaut's calm and confidence in humans as creatures of healing and help continues to bloom out of my learning to ask in ways he's able to answer, which has been key to him re-learning what was thought unlikely when he unloaded off the trailer at the beginning of his stay in my stable. He can now have the farrier work on his feet, and have his sheath cleaned without sedation. He can also have his ears touched, and a bit put in his mouth without hyperventilating. There is wonder-working power in the academic art of positive horse training.

It is important for horses to know that there is a place for them to take a deep breath inside of the questions I am asking during my work with them. It looks like them offering what they think I want and is proof of the intention with which I apply my aids. Training horses is always a conversation between nature and nurture; it is all about the horse feeling safe, and being safe, and us creating a safe space for them if it doesn't exist. If we offer horses a better way to be, they will take it every time. Mental and physical issues clear up because they know there is always light when you are with them.

#11

With horses, pressure causes tension, and tension causes resistance. From that, we get bad behavior. All of those things are the horse letting us know what we're asking them to do doesn't feel good to their body and/or mind. If we can learn to see that bad behavior starts when the horse feels pressure and not let it escalate, that's how we become better horse people, which only happens when we have the courage to be open.

There does come a time, if we practice long enough, when we come into contact with a horse, and everything we've studied and learned has absolutely no validity. I think every trainer worth their salt comes into a situation like that, and the thing that differentiates the ones who move on into the training of the horse as an art form from those who don't is understanding that when that particular horse shows up, they'll show you the answers to almost every question you've ever had if you're humble enough to listen and be changed.

#12

So, I don't look at reward as a release from work on the horse's hard side to the horse's easy side; I look at reward as me not asking anything more. I don't want the horse to loathe one side or the other, and so what I try to do is set them up in a balance on the easy side that I can try and carry over to the hard side. So I worked a lot on the left side to establish the mental structure, and then the physical structure, and then we came back around to the right and he was just right there.

This young horse being balanced in his body is predicated on him having my body in a balanced place as a point of reference. And so as long as I'm able to introduce that point of reference on the easy side, and he gets comfortable giving his body to me, he'll follow me to the hard side.

All that is to say that the answer is forward comes from calm, and straightness comes from forward. But calm comes first and always. The horse's calm is always built out of us asking them from a foundational space that is clear and decipherable and worriless. And when you've dug in the dirt to make bricks, and built the bridge to cross the canyon from hope to clarity, then the horse will begin to trust you—it's a process.

How he works is based on how he feels about the work. What he does is based on how he feels about what I'm asking him to do. And if I can work with him from the space where he feels comfortable, and safe, and he trusts me, then he will find the mental, emotional and physical balance in what I'm asking him to do. If one of his balances is missing, he's not ready for what I'm asking him to do.

And to that point, when working with a young horse, I prioritize building their confidence more than their body. So, I got him relaxed on his easy side, I have a savings account of relaxation built up that I can borrow from on the hard side. For me, it's less about a horse "doing" in the beginning, and more about setting up a place for them to be out of. That's why, if, in the beginning, I can establish the softness on the good side by spending the majority of the lesson time there, and then spend less time in softness, created on the good, on the hard side, then I've created a positive point of reference for the hard side that I can build out of. That's where time becomes the most valuable tool for the horse-human who knows how to take it, and not waste it. It's all about the mental-emotional associations we build in horses by how, and what, we ask them to do for us: If we work out of a place of peace, they will always try.

For young horses, in the beginning, it's all about the relationship, first, for me. I would much rather have a soft bend with the shoulder lifted for one circle on the hard side in the whole session than work on the hard side the whole time and have resistance. For me, that's not correct work. The softness is the key to giving the mind time to quiet down so that the body opens up. If we can move from the easy side to the hard side in a more balanced posture, that lets me know that

27

he believes in what I'm asking him to do and, more importantly, that he understands what I'm asking him to do. I use
this methodology because all of the horses in my barn have
had major traumas inflicted on their being-ness, and I have
to work from where they don't fight, and work out of where
they offer. That's how I stay in love with my work.

#13

And so today,
while I was working with Remi,
I began to think about how
if anybody's lived long enough,
there's some trauma. And how,
if we've ever been in love
with someone long enough
to not hide our hurts anymore,
and they've had the courage
to stay and see the beauty
beneath the bruises,
and how that beauty blossoms
under the sunlight of their attention,
then maybe we can kinda understand
what it's like for a rescued horse
that's found its home.

#14

It's crazy how when you ask questions in a way that they can answer them, they relax because you're clear... His relaxation is proof of your clarity. And it's understanding that classical work is built out of the horses' nature to react. They react, and so the classical work says, "I'm going to speak to the horse in a way in which it reacts when, and how, I want." Which means that I have to ask questions in a way that they can answer. I don't want horses thinking about how to respond to what's coming next. I want horses waiting to react. Because if they're in their heads, they're not in their bodies. And if they're not in their bodies, they can't answer our questions, because they can't hear us.

This is where the understanding of interspecies communication is so important. And the fact that you caught yourself wanting to over ride, the fact that you were able to observe yourself having an emotional response to where feel was lost—feel being defined as something that creates space, emotion being defined as something that takes space away. You were so caught up here that all the space was taken away. And when we're addicted to a look, we're riding emotionally.

This is where almost every dressage horse that has a training related injury, that's where it comes from. That's why mirrors are so dangerous—if we're not cultivated enough to use them, they keeps us addicted to a look. And as long as the horse looks okay, regardless of the biomechanical structure of the movement…this is where we start getting horses that retire at thirteen instead of twenty-two, or twenty-eight. There's a lot of beauty in horses that last a long time, healthily.

I was thinking about the two of you last night before I went to bed, and how, when we started working together, the three of us, everything he did was to push everything you tried to say to him out. And I remember how, when I said, "Relax your seat here," you began to explain how you spent so much time trying to get this in this place and now you're telling me to let it go!

So, I think you would then begin to understand that trainers train and teach out of a state of being. And knowledge is a syndrome like kissing spine: you have varying degrees of understanding to get the reactions from horses that you want. And the thing is, there's this battle between movements being executed, and their correct execution. Consequently, we have riders who have been taught that to get more out of their horses, they have to take, take, take, take. If we use the 'blinds opening' as a metaphor for light to come in; if you're shutting all the blinds, there's nowhere for the light to be. There's nowhere for healthy movement to go. And the degree to which you open is the degree of space you create for the opportunity to see more. A horses' healthy lightness is created by the correct allowance of space. That's why, every time that we've worked, I've introduced a different part of your body for you to focus on to create space with.

Every time we've done that, and I've come back, he's

come back in a more and more relaxed way. Which lets me know that you are clear enough for him to understand what you're asking him to do. That is classical work. When you work from that space there is no French dressage or German dressage or all that shit. It's: is the horse reacting in a way that is conducive for him to feel good enough in his body to do what you're asking him to do in a relaxed way? That's dressage.

This is the work, for you to begin seeing yourself as being able to be what he needs to answer the question you're asking. When you have permission to ride intuitively, patience automatically blooms. And to that point, I'm not coming in with an idea about what I think you should do. My only goal is to get you and your horse to hear each other better. Learning is a whole lot more interesting when you're being talked with, and not at, and where everybody's intelligence is welcomed and accepted and affirmed.

Showing is about putting everything you've learned together. Training is about taking everything you've learned apart. But, you can't put all of the pieces together correctly if you don't know what all the pieces look like by themselves, which is what we're doing. We're taking everything apart so that we can understand whatever feeling we feel is, and what it means: what it means to him and, more importantly, what he wants it to mean to you. Allowing him to go a little bit deep on the forehand, at the beginning of his lesson, calmed him down. You didn't ask him to do that. When you brought him back after a bit, he said "Here I am." That's a really important thing to know.

#15

The other day, I reread the story of the brothers, Florus and Laurus, who where taught the language of horses and the art of horsemanship by the archangel Michael. What a beautiful prayer.

When I opened my stable, my dad said I should warn against ill will and spite in my space by making a sign that says, "Only horse shit's allowed." Boundaries are the work: peaceful places must be protected and cared for with love.

This morning, as I walked towards the hay barn to start feeding breakfast to the angels, I asked them to continue teaching me the language of horses and the art of horsemanship. Amen.

#16

When you meet
a horse in need,

and it has potential,
and needs help,

and you have the ability
to help them,

and you care,
it's worth doing.

It's something that
calls to your heart.

#17

This is about trust, and if you trust yourself enough to trust your horse, that's the question. Do you trust your horse enough to allow him to carry his own body?

The answer to that question will come when you want it. Your answer will come when that question is no longer useful. But right now, why is that question valuable to you? What is the reservation to you trusting yourself, and what supports that?

Sure. Whose voice is it?

And that not being able to trust yourself is what made you second guess yourself, even when the answer is correct.

And so now we've entered into the realm of internal and external tracts of control. And so now, what is the value of your dad's voice? There's some safety there.

Ok, and how is that working?

What does small mean?

And how has it worked? It's not a question of what has it gotten you. It's a question of how has it left you feeling? Right, you've gotten what you've wanted or needed to get out of life so far. But, how has it left you feeling?

Ok. And whose on either end of the disassociation? What parts of you are on either end of the disassociation from yourself? It's kind of like the river running through the canyon cliffs: what's on either side, and who's in the middle that knows that that disassociation is actually there?

Ok. So, you said you're teetering on the edge. My question is: teetering on the edge of which cliff?

So, if you build a bridge between the overbearing father and the hurt child, what are you walking out of to walk in to? Let's just use a hypothetical, if you build a bridge over your soul from the hurt child to the father figure, what do you find when you leave the child to cross the bridge over to the father?

Yeah, it's a deep question.

Yes. So, you ran from hurt child to father figure. If you're the father figure and you run over to hurt child, what do you find?

The father figure forgiving the child?

So, which one do you want to go into the next stage as?

That's that scary space, right? Now, the bridge is from the known to the unknown, and you have to build the bridge. So, what do you build the bridge out of?

Well, and so we begin to understand that, for these horses, fear comes from that part in their training process where their understanding is lost. And that's where the work is: we get rid of the fear by teaching them how to understand what they didn't understand, which is then symbolized by behavior topped relaxation, like a freshly made, still warm, gooey, soft cinnamon bun. So, if neither one of those people is who you want to move forward as, then what part of your self do you have at your disposal to explore that scary space? Because the overbearing father and the hurt child are the only two options that you've given yourself to journey as, and you don't like either one. That's where the issue is, in realizing that you have the power to create what you want to create so that you can move forward. But, you can't create anymore than you trust.

And so the question, again: who do you move forward into the world as? Who do you move forward into that scary space as? Your faith and trust in the bridge you've built is only as powerful as the person you're crossing it as.

If your horse's back is the bridge, and you've moved from self-doubt to trust, with the posting diagonal as the metaphor, who did that?

Yes! That part of you that felt.

Focus and awareness. When we focus here, we don't feel here. When we feel here, there's trust. And it's understanding that both the hurt child and the overbearing father can trust... they can grow to trust each other. But only if they take that risk of seeing who they see when they cross the bridge form their side of the canyon to the other person's side of the canyon. And to do that, that bridge has to be made of love.

I think that's enough for today. Well done.

#18

1)
when I first met her
she was leggy,
and tall, and all fire,
and a rude,
already many-times rejected,
five-year-old
who'd been bred
to race in Kentucky
but ended up
being sold at an auction
in Nebraska
where the a kill pen buyer
was the bidder
before ending up
in a rescue in Colorado
where she was in the barn
on stall rest
for a skull fracture
after being kicked
in the head
by another horse
in the field

2)

she was eventually moved
to another ranch
and put in a huge field
with other horses
whose people
couldn't or wouldn't
love them back anymore
one day
while sunbathing in the hay
she was stomped on
by playfully galloping hooves
like cigarette butts
into a cheap motel room carpet

3)

I reached out my hand
to give her a treat
then asked if she wanted
to go home with me
I told her I was happy
the fracture in her pelvis
was nearly all healed
and that she'd be mine forever
if she wanted me
to be her person
she shot me
a look of snow
then returned
to eating her grain
from a bucket

#19

We allow horses
to have confidence
when we don't pressure them
into something
they're not ready for.
Instead of force
we let them explore it,
and we let them experience it,
and we let them ask questions of it,
and we give them time.

#20

I think of
rein contact

between
the rider's

hand and
the horse's

mouth like
Rastafari

think of
dreadlocks

as antennae
through which

they hear
God's voice

without
a bridge

there's no
connection

#21

In training horses, if the communication with them is simple, it's correct. And the more simple the work for them, the more profound it is for us. That's why correct work is so hard. The challenge and the work lay in learning how to ask questions, and hear answers, and drop the expectation and assumption that their answer is wrong, and our question is right. Horses are very honest creatures.

All this to say that, collectively, people don't give horses enough credit for their intelligence, or the depth and complexity of their inner lives. If we can open ourselves up to them in that way they'll teach us everything we need to know about them.

#22

No matter
what you do,

you can't stop
a horse

from being
a horse. That,

my dear, is
the real gift.

#23

What I'm learning to do is to say more with less. To let the horse enter the conversation with his or her own self, and opinions, and ideas, and suggestions about the work. That makes us collaborators together, the horse and me.

#24

And this is the goal of every lesson:
that they begin and end in peace.

#25

The wisdom of horses
is a path to self perfection

Horses are the path
to self-perfection I'm on

Horses are the path
to self-perfection I teach

#26

Horses get forgotten
when we stop learning

how to meet them
where they're at.

The more we learn
the more we evolve,

the more open our hearts,
the more adaptable we become,

the more horses
we're able to help

by studying different ideas,
and using science to try and create

a way of working with each one
in a way that helps him or her

learn how to feel safe
when we share space together.

This is how partnership works,
and why it's beautiful.

#27

I think one of the basics that so many people miss is making time to take care of themselves. Create time to rest, and let your body rest, and let your mind rest, and create time to do something you enjoy.

That said, I don't particularly enjoy spending a lot of time with people outside of teaching where the questions that I get stay manageable. So, I think a huge basic is self-care, and deciding what that is for you.

When it comes to teaching, I think helping people understand that their horse is not their emotional wheel barrow, and that they'd do well to learn to discipline their minds, because horses are super empathic creatures. If we're not as clear as possible about what we're bringing to the table, we're going to be fighting ourselves by way of our horses.

Also, there are rules for working with me: questions, and not knowing are super OK, and being afraid is super OK, and we can explore those things. But self-deprecation is not OK, because being open to finding that light of possibility is super-hard to find in yourself when you keep telling yourself you don't deserve it.

I think that us recognizing our own possibility, and recognizing the possibility in others, is part of what makes us holy things: to know when we are able to find the answers by trusting feel, and creating a vision for ourselves from that trust, and then walking the road towards the vision we've created, and understanding that we learn all of our lessons along the way… I think that's a really wonderful practice in unraveling what possibility is, and how, then, you can help other people be possible.

I think that, as a teacher, it's really important for me to practice saying when I really don't know the answer that "I really don't know" because it takes down my being pedestaled by students. That's something I just can't stand, when people do that to me. Equal is greater than divided.

So, I stay cognizant of my need to check-in with folks during our work together, asking them what they're feeling when they feel a change, because that's what I've learned, too: a lot of people just don't know how to feel—with horses or in life. Ninety percent of a lesson is usually spent with me travailing to find language to scalpel out how to help people find feel with.

How do I do that? Well, I'm really in touch with my body and how it holds emotion, and how it holds things, and that's come from years of practicing yoga and meditation and prayer, I think. And it's a little unfair, but I can usually feel in my body where people are holding tension in their bodies. I found that, as I'm able to go in and be more present, if I find a part of my body that is tight while I'm talking to this person, or observing this person, then I can say, "Hey, loosen up your…" or "Breathe into the back of your neck and loosen your shoulder," and it works.

My effectiveness as a teacher? I trust myself. My mom always tells me, "If you don't see the light, don't stay." My body is my filter through which I'm able to navigate the world and my work in it.

#28

So, once I went for a lesson on a friend's old-type Iberian stallion whose neck was probably bigger than my torso, and I think that he was the first horse in a long time that I had ridden where I didn't really know what to do when I was on him.

It was really interesting because my friend made the comment that she'd never seen me ride so badly in all the time she's known me. I told her that I didn't know what to do because my aids just didn't work on this horse.

He was so kind about it, which also kind of scared me because I'm used to my horses being very vocal about their dissatisfactions with me. It was one of those situations where I totally had to change how I talked to this horse to get in tune with him. She said, " Nahshon, give the right so you can get the bend."

It got to the point where I had to just ask her to please show me what she does with her body so that I could ride her horse correctly and get through to him.

Sometimes this work is personal therapy. Sometimes this work is public service. All that to say, I consider myself an alright horseman. And that even amongst the folks who are supposed to know, we still have moments where it's really, really challenging to learn new things....

It got to the point where I was a little sacred because how I'd known to use my body wasn't working, and I expressed that I was feeling a little vulnerable in the situation because I'm usually pretty accurate at reading horses.

So, not to ramble. I just thought it was important to share that because learning is important, and horses are precious. If we do it right, it's like good religion: we have the ability to work miracles. But, if done wrong, it destroys lives.

I just thought it was important to share that I'm not perfect, and that there are times that I try really hard to get through to a horse and it just doesn't work, and that's just part of the process. I'm not advocating this practice of horse-humanship, and the art of riding, and the art of learning to love horses better is a prize. For me, it is a process.

I believe in process. I believe in healing hurt spaces, and I know that the process works because I've worked with a lot of people and helped them get there, and I've worked with a lot of horses and helped them get there, and I've worked with myself and helped myself get there. And I still have a long way to go; in the process of learning how to ride, I think it's also important we continue to learn how to take care of our hearts.

That's why I love horses so much, because there's no other creature on earth, for me, that just lets it be OK for you to not have all of your shit together. They really understand if you want to be possible. And if you truly do want to be possible, they will do the best they can to help you find that light in yourself. That's why I love them.

And I've found so much joy, and so many lessons to be learned in taking my broken throwaway horses, and piecing them back together again, and seeing what stories they have to share. My horses are my best friends. When I'm with them, everything is always OK.

#29

The thing that's really important is just building a relationship with your horse, so they can trust that you're safe. My young horse, Chevy, that I had, that pinto, the first time he'd gone off the property was the first time I'd ridden him outside, and it was high up in the mountains. It was the weekend after my step-father's funeral.

So, I drove him up to the mountains—I was with some friends—to a beautiful place called Westcliffe, and he did great. But the real memorable moment of that day (I mean I hadn't introduced him to water-crossing, nothing. And he was fine, because he trusted me) was these two dogs who came running at him, off-leash, with bear-bells on (you could tell they were used to scaring horses). So they come down snarling, their bells bonging, and Chevy, I feel his body tense, I feel him ready to get-gone quick, and I lay my reins on his neck, and he takes a deep breath, and just stands there. And those dogs stopped, and they turned around, and ran away, and that was his first time out! And he was fine because we didn't do anything other than the work that we did every day. The arena is a classroom where horses learn and practice the skills that will help them stay safe and calm in the world.

A lot of us get in trouble, as horse people, preparing for new things by practicing new things. I wish I would have been humble enough when I was twenty-five to hear that doing more doesn't always get you more. Learn to do a few things right, and not a lot of things wrong. I think that's a truth that comes with understanding the value of peace, and understanding the value of keeping that peace safe.

#30

I can't guide you without your willingness to follow me. And you can't do what I ask unless you trust me.

Every lesson that happens is a two-way street for the teacher-student experience.

And that relationship that a riding teacher has with their students is the same relationship the students are learning to have have with their horses.

The job of a teacher is to teach the student how to be a teacher.

#31

He is a big, beautiful, cherry bay, rabicano Thorough-
bred with a skunk tail. I have been his person since he was
five. His registered name is Papasquiaro, maybe in honor of
the famous Latin American poet, but more likely after the
city in Mexico, which is where he was imported from. Like
some Thoroughbreds who don't make it on the track, Remi
wound up in the kill pen. He was adopted by a trainer only
to be forced to jump five foot courses as a three-year-old.
That experience left him in a gazillion little pieces, some of
which I'm still trying to find.

I first met Remi at Triples S Ranch in Fountain, Colorado where I taught dressage lessons every Friday for two
years. He was one of about six horses in a field rented from
the ranch by Safe Landing Horse Rescue for overflow, and
came running to the fence when the barn manager, Megan,
called out to him. He was broken-bodied and in need of a
person to call his own.

I visited Remi at the ranch on a weekly basis. But I didn't consider becoming his person until a few months later when I had a dream in which I was shown how to heal his hurts. The next day, I called Lanya, who runs the rescue, and told her about it. She said, "Oh my gosh, he's yours!"

A few weeks after I bought Remi from the rescue, we began our work. As his body continues to heal and his mind clears with calm, patient practice, Remi has emerged as a meticulously brilliant teacher of how horses only go to the spaces that we open for them. If all they find is closed doors, they move with closed bodies, and their minds start to follow suit. If you want a tense horse to relax, you have to try and make it possible for him to go into an open space instead of running from a closed one. We save horses by teaching them in a way that allows them to learn to feel safe in our hands.

With Remi, that took a great deal of time and patience. One of my biggest challenges was finding a bridle bit he would accept. Upon starting our training, I learned that the traditional single and double jointed snaffles made Remi bonkers. He would squeeze his eyes shut, hold his breath, open his mouth like a gaping wound, and stiffen the over-developed muscles at the base of his neck. Then he'd plant his forehand into the ground, drop his withers between his shoulders, and just start to blind bucking like a rodeo bronc. All this from trying to lead him in-hand around the arena!

We make progress when we have the courage to start over. The ability to help a horse work through trauma lives in finding those spaces in the training process where their understanding has been lost and then explaining the fear away. That is how we make difficult horses possible again—by knowing that pressure causes tension, and tension causes resistance. If we're true to the process, we see resistance as the cause of bad behavior. And we accept that horses don't resist for no reason, ever. Resistance is the horse's way of telling us that what we're asking them to do doesn't feel good.

But, knowing what questions are the wrong ones is half the battle won. Until we're willing to learn to ask horses in a way they understand, they will never give us what we want. Submission isn't submission until we submit. Remi was telling me that he didn't like the restricting nutcracker effect snaffle bits had on his tongue. So began our experimentation with bits.

My horses' teeth are kept in healthy balance by their dentist. Even still, it took me a year to find a bit bridle set up Remi felt comfortable enough to keep his tongue relaxed in and stay lifted in his shoulders, chest, and back, and breathe full-body breaths so that I could use the rein in a way that helped him stay with me.

Aside from the traditional single jointed snaffle, I tried a French link, and then a KK snaffle. The thought was that maybe the central piece laying on the tongue would reduce the nutcracker effect and lessen the direct pressure on the outside of the bars.

Though the double jointed snaffle is softer than the single jointed snaffle, they both ultimately acted on the tongue in the same way, which Remi just could not handle.

I tried a bitless bridle, too, but the pressure over the bridge of his nose from the direct rein caused him to lock his jaw and poll. He also resisted the lateral flexion, making it impossible for me to start teaching him how to bend non-forcefully. So I didn't entertain continuing to use it.

After some time I began to realize how important it is to bit a horse according to its psychology and decided on a Mylar Level 3 snaffle. The Myler system is based on tongue relief, and Level 3 is the mildest, offering virtually no tongue pressure and very little bar or lip pressure.

For Remi, it was the space he needed.

Horses only answer the question they hear being asked. The effect of the bit is only as clear as the hand on the rein. The hand on the rein is only as clear as the intention of the heart. For my work with Remi, everything flowers from the rein as a metaphor for a bridge from the known to the unknown and a safe way back, like a good poem.

#32

And this is the miracle:
I'm finding more and more horses, in my work, whose resistances are stuck in the spaces where their human's hearts
aren't open.

And this is the magic:
You know that the person's closed heart-spaces are opening
when the horse's resistances start to lessen.

Horses are direct reflections of who we are in this moment
of relationship with them. For some people, their horse is the
only honest thing in their life that lets them know that there
are some holes. Consequently, it's the only space wherein
some of those people are open to address their pain.

And this is the method:

When the horse presents an evasion, check-in with yourself and feel where it is you're not following the horse's movement to try and find what emotion your horse is using as the balance point in you to hold tension and resist.

We have emotional reactions to psychological triggers which cause physical responses. When we learn to deep-breathe ourselves beyond that cycle of non-helpful thoughts, our bodies relax enough to find feel for, and follow, our horses' bodies.

And this is the take-away:

A rider's feel for a horse is not some abstract, theoretical process or ideal. Feel is emotional discipline.

#33

Training theories are tools. I'm not an ideologue when it comes to training. The only thing that I'm against is anything that doesn't allow the horse to feel safe enough to relax when they are with me. Heart first, always. Fortunately, or not, peer pressure from dead people doesn't always fit.

All is forgiven. There's always more than one correct way. That said, I'm always open to other healthy possibilities—always. Are there any texts that you can refer me to?

I hear you. I work with a lot of horses for whom what I've read in books doesn't work. Also, I don't think it's a fair thing to assume that what I share of the work I do is all there is. There's a lot that can't be shared because words don't always work, but I'm trying.

I'm a good student. I'm a good teacher. I'm a good trainer. I'm a good listener. But, not as good as I could be if I'm given more time, and stay away from bitterness. I know how to help piece horse's and people's hearts back together again. I understand a lot of the physiology of the exercises, there are laws to how the body works. I don't have any interest in the rights or the wrongs of methods but, rather, only the truth of what horses say helps them.

Well, I would rather go in my arena and work than waste time arguing. Life's too short to be lost in anger. That said, I'm always open to constructive feedback whenever possible. I've grown a lot. I'm still growing. I'd be grateful for any text you might think would be helpful.

No. This conversation isn't hard to have, I'm not on a crusade. I agree with the correct way that you're talking about, but the texture of softness is a matter of heart, at this stage of the process, and has more to do with intention than technique. A soft, relaxed, comfortable horse is my goal, always. It's what all the horses who've wanted my help have become. Each horse has come to that place differently, though.

I'm not trying to be right, only sharing what I've found so far. We ask the questions we want answers to. Sometimes, we get the answers to the questions we've asked. Horses are honest communicators. It's also important that I acknowledge that we're sharing from different stages of individual practice. Your work deserves my respect.

As for the books, I don't speak any other European languages. English is all I've got when it comes to equestrian literature. Books are human things. But, human beings are humans beings.

#34

I've trained my eyes to trust what the horse's body tells me and to solicit the feel from a student because I can dictate the time. All of this starts from awareness—me breathing deeply in my body and trusting the feelings and the thoughts that come up in that moment. It's a co-creation between the horse, me, and the rider—that's what a lesson is. And the only way for progress to happen is if the teacher gives the student his or her presence. If I do that for you, then you learn to do that for your horse, and then your horse learns to do that for you. If I do my job correctly, then I stop being your teacher, and the horse starts being the teacher because you trust what they say. That's my job. I figure it's better job security to try and teach people how to do that than to keep them dependent on me because that's the only way I can help people grow, and hopefully help horses' lives be a little bit easier.

#35

Take 1:

You're welcome. Hey, it's okay. There's nothing wrong with needing some help... nothing wrong with needing some help. It takes a lot of courage to ask for help. That's not a lot of courage that I have all of the time, if I'm completely honest with you. Maybe I'd get more done if I were a little more brave.

What are we working on today? Slowing his motorboat trot on forehand. Alright, so what I'd like you to do is go ahead to get him warmed up however you warm him up and let me know when you both are ready.

Take 3:

Okay. So, I'm going to ask you to trust me. It's okay. So, what we're going to do is break it down. So, I would like you to stay on a twenty meter circle around me, and I would like you to just trot four or five steps. But, I want you to focus on the breath. When you focus on the breath, you come out of the muscles, and you begin to drop your guard against your horse. So, circle around me.

What's happening is that, with your trying to keep him slow, you're not breathing fully in your body. Because you're not breathing fully in your body, you're getting stiff, which is making you bounce, which is making him speed up.

Take 4:

No, I'm not going to ride him. That's a wimp out. Let me ask you this: I know what the barrier between you and him is. I can see it. But, what is the barrier between you and me? It's not an accusation. What I'm asking is, how can I help allow your fear to be a little bit smaller? You're very capable of doing that. What I want you to do, listen to me, is make everybody here disappear, and focus only on the sound of my voice. I can feel the emotion trying to take your breath away, and I want you to breathe deeply into it with emotion. And I want you to understand that I just want help you. Now, walk. Mean it. Good. Relax. We are going to break this down.

Take 7:

Slow your thighs like a funeral procession, snail mail, slow. And what I want you to do, is when you trot, just jog in your thighs. Now walk in your thighs. Good, but don't get addicted to the feeling. We're not gonna run away with it feeling good, and we're not gonna run away with it feeling bad. We're gonna build. And jog in your thighs, when you're ready. Put your shoulders over your hips, push your belly out, and walk in you thighs. You see how your seat is moving now? That's the feeling we want to keep, and you feeling how it's moving in your whole body, that's only possible because you're protracting your stomach muscles, and your back has room to think.

Take 8:

Do you feel your ischia moving up-and-down, one at a time.

And how when they're up, your rib cage shortens on that side? That's his hind legs under your seat. When your hip is up, that's his hind leg under your body, do you feel that? And do you feel how, as you're starting to feel him move your body, the worry is starting to go away? I didn't say "is gone." I said "is starting." Do you feel that? Good.

Take 9:

Now, what I want you to do is lift your heels a little bit, just a little. Did you feel how that opened the front of your hip? Good. Do you feel how your hip is moving forward-and-back? Good. Now, your thigh is moving forward and back at the same time that his corresponding shoulder is moving forward and back, do you feel that? Good. Now, when the thigh is back, the hip, and stirrup are down, do you feel that? Good. Now, when the stirrup is down, step into it. Good. Now, step heavier and longer. Good. What did he just do? Yes, he gave you a bend and he slowed down. Good. Now, lighten your steps. What happened? Yes, he sped up. Good.

Take 10:

What's happening when his trot gets motor-boaty, is that you're bracing with your thighs. I know that because the weight in the stirrups is light. If you've ever galloped a horse whose been trained to gallop correctly under a rider, they speed-up when you come out of the saddle. As soon as they feel your butt in the saddle, they slow down. It's the same thing with him, he's going fast because your thighs are lifting your seat off of his back, does that make sense? And this is from you trying to hold a proper dressage leg position. So, we're going to do the opposite of what we did for everybody else today, open your knees and toes out a little bit. Good. See, sometimes we can make a thing right when we know what is wrong. Very good.

Take 10:
Stop self-deprecating, and take credit for the beautiful work that you're doing. This isn't good luck, this is good technique. Self-deprecation is one of the biggest hindrances to progress. This is what I want you to do, I want you to give yourself more credit for what you're doing. You are doing this, enjoy it. Because you have just overcome a whole lot.

This lets you know that the fear you were holding, the apprehension that you were holding, was because you didn't understand. And when it was explained in a way in-which you could understand, you know how to ask the question to receive the answer you're asking for. The question is the answer.

Take 11:
Stay present and enjoy the beauty of the process: this is the art of relaxation. It allows you to feel by you giving yourself room to think, so you can respond instead of react. You're not being held hostage by fear, but you're using fear to teach you how to not be afraid.

Take 12:
You got it. It is a rhythm. It's a dance, yes. You got it! You got

it! You. Don't. Get. It. Unless. You. Move. It is a rhythm. It's a rhythm like the breath is a rhythm. It's a rhythm like fear is a rhythm. And you can't get into it if you're in your head. You can't get into it if you try to create it. You can only get into if you follow, right? Now you're groovin'. Go-'head, go-'head, go-'head. Good job. Beautifully done.

Take 14

That's right, stirrup stepping keeps the butt from doing it's thing. Try this, step down slow. Did you feel your toes spread out? Good. When you spread your toes out, did you feel the back of the knees soften? No? Okay, try it again. Step: do you feel, the back of the knee's soft? Yes, good. That softens the hip flexor. The hip flexor being soft allows the lower abdominal muscles to protract, which allows the lower back to follow the horse's hind legs, which allows you to sit independently in the saddle.

Take 15:

Yeah, you were trying to loosen the hip flexor with your toes closed, and you unknowingly locked the tendons and ligaments behind your leg, which allowed him to interpret the flexed quadricep as driving aid.

Take 16:

Now, let your arms follow his neck, it doesn't mean shorten the rein. It just means be mindful of his movement. Good. There, now you're groovin'.

35

Take 17:

Riding is very foreign for us, anyway. And people don't do well understanding foreign things if they don't have a point of reference to use as a metaphor. We need a bridge from the known to the unknown and a safe way back. That's the job of a metaphor. So if you use the horse's back moving your seat as a metaphor for how we move when our feet are on the ground, when we're walking on the horse, we're walking on the ground. When we're trotting on the horse, we're jogging. When we're cantering on the horse, we're skipping… and you can step.

Take 18:

Yep, getting hung up on the look fucks everything up. Just like getting hung up on how someone speaks prevents you from hearing what they're saying. Good, now to weight your seat bones down, bend your arms and make your elbows heavy.

Take 19:

You want to do everything right, because you're afraid of doing it wrong, which is why you're always at war with yourself. But, there's no need for war. There's no need for anyone to win or lose.

Take 20:

It is simple, that's what makes it so hard. And I think people are better than just wanting to make things so hard that it's impossible to get correct. People mess up so much because we don't understand what we need not to mess up, and we want it so bad that we don't take the time to understand so we don't mess it up.

Take 21:

Okay, this is what I want you to do: really make sure that your pinky toes are spread open. No, don't force your whole foot. I didn't ask for the ankle, I just asked for the pinky toe. Do you feel how it softened your groin muscle? Yeah, and did you feel how his back just lifted up into the inner-thigh. Yeah, there you go. Very good.

Take 22:

He looks like he's actually enjoying this. Yeah, I agree, now that you're not squeezing him to death. He says, "Touché." But, it doesn't have to be the end of the world if we don't understand what we want to understand. That's why I was saying at the beginning how profound of a thing it is for you to have the courage to ask for help. Because that's what this is, and that's a really, really hard thing to do: to open up your body in the way that you want your horse to open up his body. So, thank you. It's good to see you happy on your horse, and your horse happy with you on him. Good work.

Take 23:

Yes. Well, the job of a teacher is to bend to how each students learns so that each students can find their light, too.

#36

So, today the vet came to give my horses their fall shots, and when we got to Remi, I told the vet how we'd just made a video of him yesterday about using the piaffe as a tool for relaxation and how it was the movement I taught him first to start building his body up.

He said, "Piaffe, You started at the back door, didn't you? How did you know to go there first?"

"I listened to him," I said.

"And how did you know what he was saying?"

"I don't know," I said. "He just relaxed. That was the space he was willing to let me into."

"You met him be where he was at," the vet said. "Like Jesus."

I looked at him a bit bemused.
"I'm a Christian," he continued. "Jesus meets us where we're at."

"I don't know much about Jesus," I said. "Except that he was a gentleman most of the time and he thought religion was for people and not people for religion. That's how I feel about dressage," I said. "It's for horses, not the other way around. And what it has allowed me to do, effectively, is isolate parts of the body to set off a chain reaction of engagement in the horse.

So, I lifted his thoracic spine, which flexed the hips. When the hips flexed, the lumbar spine lifted. When the lumbar spine lifted, the stifles flexed. When the stifles flexed, the cervical spine softened. When the neck softened, the hocks flexed. When the hocks flexed, the jaw flexed. When the jaw flexed, the poll softened. That's how I unlocked this horse.

#37

Sometimes, those parts of our past we've buried (way deep down in the bottom of the dark where light does not reach and leftover voices occur) bubble up into the lives we bring to our horses and change how we see what we see when we see. Last week, at the end of a lesson with one of the people who studies with me, I brought up the fact that every time I asked what she felt, she answered with what she thought and began to explain the reason why. In the midst of her voice I interrupted (gently) and asked if she thought the reason was worth sharing that she please write it down and give it to me next week.

Today, after our lesson, I went into the hay barn, sat on the tractor, read what she wrote, and wept as I made my way across the page, one word after the other up to the end. It began: "When you asked me what I was afraid of, I suddenly knew what it was, but there is no way I could voice it." When I finished, I went for a walk, dried my tears, and thought about how the space trainers hold for students is invisible until it isn't, and how that space can only do one of two things: help or hurt.

I returned to the stable, brought Remi out of his stall, took him to the wash bay to prepare him for his piaffe lesson in-hand, while I described what I'd just read, then asked him what it meant. He looked at me with his beautiful eyes and said, "You heal what you forgive."

I once read that help is when you find an answer that's better than the one you have. I'm thankful for my horses.

#38

So this is what my lessons with students have brought me to the understanding of, as it pertains to my role as a teacher:

Me to my student: "I give you permission to give yourself permission to try and do what I ask you to do. If you do it, great. If not, great. But if you don't, let's stay there—that's where the lesson is."

This, in-turn, teaches the student how to hold the same space for their horse that I hold for them, and, strangely enough, empathy begins to blossom, and the horses don't feel so misunderstood because their riders don't feel so misunderstood. The journey. This is as far as I've gotten.

#39

When the student says to the teacher, "This doesn't feel right. This is what I'm feeling." The teacher would be wise to acknowledge that. A student having the courage to do that lets me know that they are not afraid. And that they feel safe enough with me to say, "What you just suggested didn't work."

The job of a great teacher is to teach teachers. What happens between me and my student needs to eventually happen between my student and their horse. If they can't correct me and say, "That suggestion did not work," how can they do that with the horse when horses only answer the questions they hear being asked.

What is the goal? To have people be in better relationship with their horses. I'll do almost anything to try and make that happen.

#40

We gather all of our intelligence in our brains, but we don't trust it in our bodies. Yes, we can use the mind as our voice speaking to the horse, but only if we use the body as an ear to listen to what the horse hears us saying. Then, it turns into a beautiful conversation and exchange of ideas, and the horse can teach you how it likes to be ridden.

And this is the gift: once we move into the heart-space of respecting a horse's sentience, they begin to teach us a lot about healthy growth, because all we then are able to do with them is listen. If we take behavior as language, when they are calm and relaxed, we know we've done something right. When they're spooked and anxious, something must be changed. Peace is the horse's true nature, and if we don't have that while working them, then something is not correct.

And here is the beauty of horses: when we come to them with an open heart and respect for their intelligence, they lead us to a place where we find the courage to be better people. And for me, personally, realizing that my horses are making a choice to allow me into their energy, and to trust me to hold their questions in my hands and help them find answers—that is the world.

Dressage is medicine for horses when it's not a bad circus act.

Horses don't break down when the work is correct. And if they are broken down, if we can get them to a place of correct work, and they want to, they heal.

#41

There are many things
to do with a horse. But,

there's only one way
to be with a horse,

and that's in love.
They understand

that language very clearly.
It keeps our intentions pure.

#42

He calls her "Ms. Shalam,"
and says that her voice lives
in the right side of his chest
telling his heart it'll all be okay
when he feels afraid.

This little boy is a genius
with his ability to feel.
His mare, a saint.

#43

This evening my niece came over because she told my sister that she needed to come to her Princess Farm and get all of the extra energy out of her body so that she could find her listening ears again—because she'd lost them.

I asked her why it was important that she find words to tell her mommy what she needs, and how she feels. She said, "So Mommy can hear me. When Mommy hears me, she knows what's happening to me. When Mommy knows whats happening to me, she can help me."

"I try to do for the horses what your mommy does for you," I said.

She said, "Yeah."

#44

Healed horses help heal hurting human hearts.
Healed human hearts help heal hurting worlds.
Black lives matter in my barn.

#45

look at all
of the memories
in our bodies

and the reasons
for them
to be there

that we must
work through
and let go of

to find
freedom
in ourselves

#46

I have a problem existing without horses. So my solution for existing is to work with horses: they allow me the liberty to be awake while offering me dreams.

This afternoon while working with Ms. Shalam, in-hand, I asked her to bring the front of her back hooves to the back of her front hooves so that she could stretch her back, before she knelt down on bent knees as if in prayer then looked up at me and asked, Do you want me to lay down?

I stood there feeling feelings I didn't understand how to feel. I'd never had a horse offer this. Nor had I ever read about teaching a horse to kneel (from Goat on the Mountain Top) without hobbles, or ropes, or taking the horse's body away from the horse, which is why I've never tried.

The unreality, and the truth, of it all.

Simplicity is such an unknown wonder.

#47

We are a commodity-driven society where it's rare to find people who can find value in something others see as worthless. If, as a teacher, I do my best to try'n help people open doors in their hearts that have been closed, their horses will change for the better. In the beginning, dressage was part of the development of noble people. It was part of the educational curriculum. I think in understanding that the foundation of this work lies in producing better horses by producing better people, we are able to see that correct work with horses is a really wonderful way of healing the human heart, and healed human hearts are a really wonderful way of helping heal a hurt world.

#48

Only horse shit is allowed in my barn.

#49

Today, in the lunge lesson with Ms. Shalam and her little boy, we began working on the hand and elbow position to start teaching him how to earn reins, and the correct position of his back and belly so that he could begin to learn the magic of his seat. He'd mastered doing "Around the World" at the walk, "Helicopter," and lifting straight legs up over his mare's neck and touching his feet together. Right now, his lessons only last about 30 minutes.

Anyway, in between sets of walk-trot transitions with his seat, I asked him how his body felt. He said, "Focused." Then I asked him how his mind felt. He said, "Clear." Then I asked him to explain. He said, "I can feel Ms. Shalam's movement. Riding my horse with my listening back is giving my mind room to think."

All I could do is smile and say, "Yes."

There is a beautiful passage, Tao Te Ching 27, that says, "Those who arrive at their destination teach those who are still on the path, while those still on the path are a source of inspiration for the teachers."

#50

My biggest challenge is that, sometimes, when I present the information, you just decide that it doesn't work because you don't want it to. And then you get upset because I have her working well, because I know what I'm doing, and I'm trying to help you find it so that you're not struggling so much.

I'm just saying that half of the challenge of why you're feeling so hopeless with your horse is because there are things that you've decided should work for her that aren't working. She works well for me because I ask her what works for her, and I change for her. She can't find softness if the only thing you're teaching her to is fight: the whole issue with you and this mare is her mouth, your hands, and your seat. Your seat is getting better.

All I'm saying is that I'd much rather you talk with me and try, or at least entertain, what I'm asking you to do, than create this polarity of 'She works well for you, but not for me, and I'm gonna ask you to ride her like I ride her with no spurs and no whip, and with my saddle instead of yours…' I don't need the spurs and the whip. I don't abuse horses to get them to do what I'm asking them to do.

I can ride this horse in anything. But, she's yours, not mine. I'm trying to prepare her for you. But, for it to work, you can't keep purposely deciding that she needs what she keeps telling you she doesn't need. When you listen she doesn't spook.

All I'm saying is that she works better for me because I give her what she says she needs from me and not what I thinks she needs me. That's why you hired me. She's getting better because I'm listening to her.

No. She's not hot with you because she needs me to work her more, she's hot with you because you're not taking seriously how I'm trying to teach you to communicate with her in the way that she's teaching me that she understands. It's all about understanding.

This is how she works for me because I trust myself and I trust her. That's it. As long as you feel like you have to protect yourself against her, she's gonna feel like she has to protect herself against you, and resist you like you resist her. She's only doing what's you're doing.

You want the lightness, but you're not giving her the tools she needs to reach it for you. She doesn't need your pampering as a reason for why she should work for you. She takes the clarity you bring as a member of our team as a reason she should work for you. When you're clear, she is soft. When you just keep buying her more stuff, but don't speak in a way she understands, all that other stuff doesn't matter.

That's the thing about this horse. When you're afraid of her spooking, she spooks. When you're not afraid of her not spooking, spooking isn't the focus of your work with her, then she works. She's not getting a double-bind message. She's an embodiment of your mind.

It has nothing to do with tack, unless it doesn't fit. It has to do with how we're asking her to do what we're asking her to do: I'm asking her to stay with me, not to not run away from me. And because my connection with her is the single point in my mind, she focuses.

The clarity is in my allowing her to move forward. She can't find her balance if she has nowhere to go. It seems, it feels, like there are times when we make brilliant progress, and you feel the change, and you become afraid of the progress you've made, and you try and run back. When will running back stop being a useful option for you? Why are you so afraid of having a healthy relationship with your horse when you work so hard for it?

It's not figuring out how to keep her from spooking; it's you allowing yourself the courage to allow her to move forward without the fear that she's gonna run away. That's the work. That's the only thing. You are capable physically, you are capable intellectually, but there's this emotional sticking point that you're refusing to accept that you can give yourself the permission to be free of, and it shows up every time you make progress.

Every time you get better, you stop feeling like you're getting better. And part of it is because you're looking for something instead of feeling for something. If you feel it, you can see it, but if you look for it, you'll never find it. Then you come in in these moods where you're not satisfied, and it keeps you blind to the effort your horse is offering, and so you just push her into feeling like she has to defend her hind legs from your hands. She can't offer you work any healthier than the space from which you're asking her.

It was even like when I asked you not to video your lesson. You asked, "What am I doing to get her to relax? I don't know what I'm doing." You're not thinking about what it's going to look like. You're just feeling it, and in that moment, you saw it, because you were present. Outer order comes from inner-calm. I can only help you to the extent that you're willing to follow my suggestions. But, when you get tired of the structure and feel like you need to have everything your way, you just get stuck again, and I can't help you out if you don't listen to me.

You're not giving yourself enough time. You need patience. I've been working with her on the same thing for a year, too, and look at how much better she's gotten. Why do I feel like I have to keep fighting with you about me knowing what I'm doing when it comes to training your horse? I'm saying, "This is what I need from you," and you come up with all of these excuses...

If you do what I ask so that I can teach you how to feel what I'm feeling when I ride her, why won't you allow me to do that? That's key. Every time I try it, though, you just decide that this is not what you want to do. You try by yourself what I do when you watch me ride, and you use that as evidence as to why it doesn't work, and you don't give me a chance, and that's the hole you're digging for yourself.

That was the first flying lead change she's done under saddle, because we've been working on the same thing for a year. The basics are everything.

#51

and this
is the secret
to helping horses

listen to them
more than you
talk to them

allow them
to hear
themselves

they will
appreciate
the friendship

#52

And now you see how you can turn really deeply conditioned evasive behavior into really brilliant work by sculpting it with a well-focused, intentional response. But, you can only do that if you're not afraid of losing.

If you're afraid of losing, then you fight to win. To win means something has been taken away. So we don't take anything away. Instead, we offer something.

When our aids aren't the brutish henchmen of some totalitarian dictator, they're invitations. "Join me here, please?" "How can I help make you happy?" That's what an aid should be. Not, "You must listen."

Reframing our aids as helpers of horses changes our minds. It makes you become really creatively clear in how you communicate with your horse.

I'm really proud of you, kiddo. This is really brilliant work that you're doing. Now, what we're gonna do is put words to all the tools that you have so that you know when, where, why and what for, and the degrees therein.

You have this rare ability to not be afraid. And because you're not afraid, you're not afraid of not having control, which makes what you say to her very, very, very, very, very clear, which makes her feel safe.

That's key to bringing broken horses back to harmony: you know how to listen.

But you've got to continue to get the emotional part right so that there's space for you to feel, because feel is the most courageous thing that you can do. When you do that, you're open to new ways of understanding how horses hear screams, but listen to whispers.

#53

we (horses
and humans)

must bend
to learn life

if we don't
we stay stiff

inelastic
unchanged

fear fighting
freely forward

is karma
resisting change

#54

The Student: To be one with the horse,
the horse must follow you.

The Teacher: To be one with the horse,
you must follow the horse.

#55

catch the horse
doing something right
in the your work with them
and praise them
    praise them
    praise them
so they begin
to trust you enough
to try and offer
what they think
makes you happy

    and also
so that when
you clarify your questions
they don't feel like
they need to
protect themselves
from your help

#56

the horses in my barn
always arrive very damaged

so much so that I never know
if they'll ever come back around

but I've accepted that they're here
for me to try and help

and that if they want help
they'll show me the way

#57

What I want you to do, because I can feel the agitation, is to just start on the ground. So, lead him on a circle.

Find your breath. Just like we do when we're riding. I want you to pay attention to the breath, to the feeling of it coming in and out of your body.

When he does that, acknowledge it by taking a deep breath, and softening. The ice sliding down off the roof is a scary thing. But, what makes you breathing into his behavior a useful exercise is that when he reacts, you have the choice to respond, and then how to respond, instead of just freezing (and in this weather, that's really easy to do. Corny joke!)

That's it. Breathe. Just breathe. Perfect. And because he didn't feel you lock up, he didn't have anything to balance his silly reactivity off of. He's very much feeding off the energy you're allowing yourself to share.

So, what I want you to do is remember something that makes you feel safe, and hold that space in your mind, and breathe into that space. Allow that space to help allow your body to relax when you feel safe. Good.

Now, fill the arena up with the feeling. Just let it out, slowly. And when the tinge of fear, or concern pops up into the body, acknowledge it by breathing into it. Let it be there in your awareness, but don't focus on it enough to take you out of your safe space. There.

When you can manipulate the energy, you can work miracles.

That's it. Breathe, yes. Breathe, yes. Let the skin at the back of the neck relax down. It'll soften the inside tops of the scapula, right at the base of the neck. There.

Let the skin on the outside of the arms soften, and drape down, and fall, like the ice off the roof. Yeah, you're getting it.

Be sure to keep the toes as soft as you can, I know it's a little bit hard, sometimes, when it's cold. But, so the quadriceps stays soft, and the stride stays long, and so your belly stays soft and fills with the breath… That's it.

Let the skin on the inside of the arms relax, and let the relaxation flow down into the palm of your hands, into the rein. Breathe into it. Soften the glutes. Very good. Warm the safe space up… Keep it warm. Brilliant.

Relax the jaw, tongue to the roof of the mouth, so that the breath goes in and out of the body slowly… slowly and fully. So that then you can begin to identify those deep down spaces where the thought of, "What if everything goes to shit?" are. Breathe into it. But watch it pass. Breathe into the spaces that that thought makes tense.

Put the tongue to the roof of the mouth so that face softens, and the chest opens, and the spine lengthens. Very good. Your horse is a meditation master. Very good. Very good. Yes.

Where are you at in your body?

More relaxed.

It's moving, yeah. Any energy that doesn't need to

be there, be mindful of it, and release it, let it go. Eliminate what doesn't evolve you. That's the work.

Soften the eyebrows, and the forehead. Let the skin on the face soften, and lengthen. Let the ears relax and open. Yeah, good. Let the breath expand your torso, front and back, and to the sides, and in-between. Let it open up your body.

The elbows, breathe into them. The bottoms of your feet, breathe into them. That's it. The palms of your hands and the tips of your fingers, breathe into them. That space between the armpit and the rib cage, breathe into it.

The iron wall that is fear, is really a curtain made of silk. On the other side off the bad-memory-filled anxiety is you, wholly reborn and continuing on...

The beauty of being a human being is that human beings are always possible. Possibility is the light. When we are present, we don't have to be afraid of the future. And when we are present, we can forgive the past. Staying aware of being here, now, makes you one of the most powerful human beings in the earth. Why? Because you can create whatever you want this moment to be by what you choose to focus on, and what you choose to be aware of. Like my three-year-old niece says, "Information is my super-power." Choices are magic things.

What a magnificent horse you are Mr. G. Mr. G. says, "I know."

That's the power you have. When you stop seeing yourself as something other than your horse, your horse stops being something other than you, to you. But, to him, you're always with him, when you're with him. Which is how you were able to do what you just did: you made him feel safe, by being safe. You let him know that he didn't have to be concerned with the ice falling off the roof if you weren't.

Horse and rider in harmony: $1+1=1$.

#58

1)

Today feels like a the final act in a three act play about him seeing you, and showing you who are, and you changing so that he feels safe in your hands. So hold that space. Hold that space, because for the longest time the halt was impossible. This is the most vulnerable place he could be right now. Now we're starting to find it.

So, what happens is we'll have a few seconds of that trust...
    And then it runs away, yeah.
    And then it runs away.

Do you remember that lesson where we were doing posting diagonals, and every time you went off into the trot, you started on the correct diagonal, but then you switched because you didn't trust yourself enough to trust him? And you got to that point to where we built that bridge between the Overbearing Dad and the Hurt Kid, and found this space where you decided who you wanted to move forward in life as, and that how, then, you began to trust yourself enough to trust him. Now, you're opening up that space for him. Does he trust himself enough to trust you? You've proven yourself worthy to be trusted. You've kept showing up, you've slowed down, and you've schooled him at the pace that he's needed to get to the place where he chose to feel safe enough for you to help him heal his hurt, too.

2)

Halt. Let the rein out. Good.

> How does it feel to hold this space?
> *He was really in a vulnerable circle. I'm not sure I have words for it.*
> Why did he allow you into that space?
> *Well, what I've learned is just, at the halt, that what he requires is so much more subtle than I have ever been able to offer before today.*

Right, and the more subtle you are, the more trusting he is. But, when the trust in you gets too close to his heart, he just armors up again. He tries to leave his body to get you to leave your body. So, when we hit that armored-up space, we just come back to the halt and work on that subtly again, and we work on him, first, finding the feel.

Feel being defined as you speaking to him without worry, right? You asking him in a way in which your question reflects your intention. It has to be a whole-self question. You can't ask one thing with your body and another thing with your mind. It has to be all-right-here-now. In the now, judgement's gone. In the now, fear is gone…all the shit that makes us armor up is gone. It's that bare-soul space. To get him to trust being bare souled with you, you have to stay in that space.

3)

Halt. Yes. Good.

How many times have I felt we were starting over? This is like learning how to steer a horse in a whole different way.

Yeah. But, here's the thing: when it's true, we're always at the beginning, again. Each moment has its birth, life and death. If you can build the work out of that space, out of that presence, you make tremendous progress.

Soften your hands forward a little bit. Did you see how he just unlocked his poll? Good, opening left rein. Close the fingers and open the left arm... and walk. Soft. Good. Halt. Everything stops... Turn him. He's trying to take it up. Good, squiggly lines. So, now turn right. Just soft feel. Yep, now left. Ahhh, yeah!

Where is the anger coming from?

I don't know. There's nothing to resist against.

There. So, when he's angry like that, breathe in to it. Don't try to take it away. Breathe in to it. Breathe in to it. Keep your body soft, but poised. Set a fair boundary. And walk a little bit, a few steps... The world would be so different without trauma, wouldn't it?

4)

And halt. And halt.

What's he saying?

I don't know what the anger piece is.

Let me sit on him.

It's piss and vinegar. I don't know if he's saying, "We're going to a place…"

"…that I don't want to go." Yeah, that's what it's feeling like.

"You're taking me somewhere that I don't want to go."

Let's switch.

Thank you.

Yep.

5)

Good.

Are you seeing anything?

So, what comes up is when he was first started. The adult who first sat on him, there's something there.

What is it? You're on to it.

He was so over-ridden.

You're finding it. Keep giving voice to it. You're walking him through.

They were protecting themselves from him. He didn't understand what anything they were asking him meant. He was not wanting to be told what the fuck to do.

By who?

By whoever was on his back.

What was their fear? What were they protecting them-selves from him for? What were they running from?

Themselves. They were running from themselves, and so the way to do that is to make the horse run…

Did you see what just happened when you said that? He just hurried off.

I did. I'm watching it all… and they punished him for not understanding by just making him run. By just doing too much.

Okay. So, we're opening up this energy. So, what did they need to do?

Nothing. They just needed to stop, and do nothing, and just sit on him for little but to let him at least try to figure out what they wanted.

And how would that make him feel?

Heard.

Heard. And, what would he say to them?

He'd say, "Please, just let me try and figure out how to be here."

6)
Good.

What's coming up?

It's a little, tiny, dark circle.

Okay? What's the reason? There's no light?

Years of walling out.

Years of walling who out? Walling as a verb….

Yeah. Yeah yeah. yeah.

Walling WHO out?

I'm not sure who is the question. Walling out the feeling. It's a form of denial like, what if we face the feeling that it hurts to feel…?

If you walk into a dark room, and the light is only there because you you are. What does that mean? Again: If you walk into a dark room, and the light is only there because you are. What. Does. That. Mean?

That I am the light.

7)

And this is the magic, that when you face that fear, and you have the courage to un-wall what you have been walling, the only thing you find on the other side of that lost piece of yourself that's been waiting for you on the other side. Then what happens is the work of changing, of habituating healthier habits, begins.

Habituating healthy habits…?

It begins. Because, though you've found that new space, you trust the walls.

Right.

And you've learned to trust that dark space.

Right.

And you've learned how to live without that lost part of yourself you now have. For him, that looks like proper lateral flexion, and proper following of feel, instead of feeling like he has to take your hands away in order to make sure you're safe enough not to hurt him. Not you, particularly. Just, hands on the rein. Because this is everybody's hands until we start using them in a different, more helpful way. We don't order, we ask. Consequently, he softens.

I think that's what people don't understand, is that holes in understanding, in both horses and people, have more than just physical consequences, they have major, major emotional and mental consequences, too. Because the body is nothing more than a memory held in the present. And memories are thoughts, and thoughts are the mother of emotion.

What does my first step look like around growing new habits that don't have to do with my first response is pulling.

That's the first step: understanding that pulling is your first response. To fix an issue you must first identify it, right?

8)

This is what I'm beginning to understand: we can't intentionally try not to traumatize horses until we've begun healing our own selves, because there's this helpful intention, and then there's the unconscious mind producing all this not-so-helpful karma that we don't know about. When we bring that stuff to the surface, then we begin to see, when we have the courage to not run from it anymore, what's really going on.

And this is the thing about running: you can only run for so long until you get tired. Then what do you do? What do you do when you've been running from your own shadow, with your back to the sun, before you turn around and that light is all you see?

9)

Good work. Any questions?

Where do I begin?

By naming it, I think. By identifying certain behaviors that he does that trigger you. Because this is him moving towards a space that is comfortable because it's familiar, a functional disfunction. The technique that we use is built out of what we trust, and that's what we reinforce: where is home.

Right.

If home is a little dark dot… What questions are in that space to be answered? That's the starting point. I'm continuing to wall myself off, why am I doing that? How is this helping me? Because, this is how I'm going through the world, and it's affecting how I see what I'm seeing, and I'm building a life out of the walled-off, little black dot that I've allowed myself to become.

#59

Wait! Don't give anything up. But, don't take anything more. Inside hand by the thigh, and you just hold it there. Breathe. Inside hand down. He's trying to push you out of the way. Now, offer the rein to the side of the neck. Inside rein down. Down. Release. Yes.

So we're going to hold the anger, and we're going to redirect it into something beautiful. Yes, there. And straight.

You see, now he's only thinking about throwing a tantrum. He's not throwing it because now you know how to unlock his body without being emotionally attached to his behavior. Yes. There, did you feel the change in his chest? Yes. Praise him. That's beautiful. Good, let him walk...

So, this is the energy of unconditional love with boundaries. And because you're fair, and because you're not fighting, he learns to trust it. Something very important just happened: he caught himself before he allowed himself to lose control, because he knew he had your support in a way that was helpful. That's what it's all about.

This behavior, running off as resistance, it starts in the very beginning when they're young because they don't understand, and they're punished for not understanding. And so, he gets to a place where he's like, "She's asking me to be vulnerable, and I really don't understand how to be vulnerable, so I'm going to do everything I can that will keep me away from having to do that because the last time I was soft like this, and I wasn't sure, I remember it not feeling so good."

But at the heart of the temper tantrum was the fear of vulnerability, and when you understand that, you're saying "Don't be bothered," you're asking to allow you to help him resolve what's bothering him. That's a more helpful place to work from. It's unfair to ask them to not be bothered.

And instead of getting annoyed with him, your answer to that behavior was, "This is what relaxation feels like in this moment, and if you follow me, I can make sure you get there. And I'll wait. Right? And that's the energetic aspect of it; when our work with horses is about us, we glorify the prize. When it's about the horse, we glorify the process. And because horses don't care about time, our super-power is patience. Good training takes the time it takes.

What he's feeling is valid, and he should be feeling it, but it shouldn't be the end of the world. That's all I'm saying.

...and to really have the courage to sit with it, and understand why you're bothered by what's bothering him, and allow him to explore too without any expectation of...

Life changes when you don't allow force to be an option. Force is predicated on fear, and fear is a prison. You can't trust a horse trained with force. They're gonna wait for any chance they can get to challenge that.

So, that's why, if we look at logically how horses process information when we're asking them to do something, opening the outside heel is a lot better than kicking with the inside leg for a leg yield...

And that moment, over there, that was from him expecting you to say go forward and stay back, but you opened a door, and he lifted his shoulders, and his hind legs came beautifully under his body, and you created a new point of reference because you didn't allow yourself to resort to force as a weapon. And you taught him, in that moment, how to find freedom in his body. That was beautiful. That was gorgeous. Freedom is a beautiful thing.

Good. Now, show her how to feel safe for her until she knows how to do it for herself. Good.

So we're just gonna hold the space for her. It's doula-ing in the truest sense. Yes. Look at how her stomach is engaging. Good.

Now I want you try and recognize her best try. It doesn't have to be the best execution, just the best try. Good. And reward her. It's good that you see she's trying. That's one of the secrets to piecing broken horses back to wholeness again.

You see how softness led to relaxation led to lightness?

Good, now you're talking to her.

Take all the time you need. And this is the thing to understand: that there's a very human-centered way of working with horses, and there's a very horse-centered way of working with horses.

In the person-centered way of working with horses, there's never enough time. And so we've got to get everything way, way, way done yesterday. Horses are ruined by the person-centered way because people are too impatient to have anything less than expectations and competition and emotion. It's really hard for people to be kind to themselves in this pretty-looking way of living.

In the horse-centered way of working with horses, time doesn't exist, and things happen quite quickly because you're not working within the realm of time. Past and future don't exist. You're only working in the now—that eternal space. And when you have that, when you have forever, you make tremendous progress by allowing yourself the space to explain each step, and each step within each step, because eternity, the preset moment, it doesn't last that long... answers are found by trusting what we feel.

And because you're not working out of that human space of trying to get her soft, she's offering it to you. And because she's offering you softness, she's light: her energy is lighter, her eyes are gentle and warm, and she's relaxed.

And so it's important to see that when she comes in to her lesson super-super-super amped up, she's sensing peopleishness, she's sensing timetables, and expectations.

In order to stay, allow yourself to stay possible on this journey to the horse, it's important that you hold these three jewels close to your heart, always: 1) Is learning how take all the time you need, so you don't waste the time you have; 2) Is knowing that memory is the mother of forgiveness; and 3) Is remembering that another day is another chance.

Good lesson today. We're all done.

#60

It's really easy to forget that everything a horse does with people, they've learned from people. When we get a horse who has been broken in some way, it's important to realize that there are some hurts that we can't heal. But, if we're able to find the soft space inside of the resistance and we can work around it, then other people's mistakes don't really matter.

My horse Nova will never be a fixed horse. But, he is able to be retrained, which will take me forever. I'll always be learning which buttons not to push to put him back into behaviors everyone hated him for. Which he still reverts to, occasionally, when he's feeling insecure, or when he doesn't want to do what I'm asking. And when he doesn't want to do something, I respect the fact, and we do something else, and he's usually willing to do it later in the lesson. And if not, then we give it another go when I'm able to ask in a way that helps him feel more safe inside of the question. Regardless of how long ago, or the brilliant progress he has made since our love affair began, those really panic-pained parts of his past are never too far away. Evermore, we carry on, gently and increasingly aware.

This is a relationship in which my body is nothing more than a fragile parenthesis in the midst of a horse's move-ment. A camaraderie transforming my intentions into something more beautifully simple, and of undisputed origin. All I want is to be is a worthy student of horses so that I can help make the world a better place for them. Invariably, this means trying to teach people that horses aren't microwave dinners, or ever to blame for what they hear us asking.

Working with horses in this way will change you, it shines out into the world from your heart. It's a really interesting practice to live out of that soft space. When you do, you begin to see new parts of yourself being born. Parts that you never knew weren't there because you didn't have eyes to see them. Horses have the ability to grow people in that way. They've taught me how to create worlds I want without feeling like I have to escape the worlds I don't. When I have a horse who's been abused, or mistreated enough to feel like they have to protect themselves from people, I don't try to teach them how to not be afraid but, rather, how to help them let me hold what they're afraid of. Horses are afraid of losing control of their bodies, just like people are.

If we push and pull with no release, or tactlessly, and it doesn't kill them, horses sink into learned helplessness, trauma-induced behaviors where they're either over-reactively hot, or under-reactively cold. This is how they hide from the pain of improperly-put-on pressure. The middle way is the way of calm, forward, and straight horses and the people who've taken the time know how educate them correctly. The fruit of properly-applied horse training technique is trust, not obedience. Peace and understanding, not performance. Presence, not absence. Feel, not fear.

Feel is different things for different people. Oftentimes, it lives in the mysteriously etherial energy high up in the hills of some mythical place like Atlantis or Shangri-La beyond the straightjacket of wise words and sound-minded thoughts and modernity. But I need guidance, and meditation and present day. So, for me, feel speaks purposefully, plainly, and to the point without worry. Feel is being naturally aware of your body language and subtle messages. Feel encourages those around you. Feel responds instead of reacts. Feel speaks in a way that is loving, honest, and helpful. Feel knows when to speak and when to stay quiet. Feel is aware of how questions reflect intention. Feel stays engaged while listening. Feel expresses you in a way that others can be attentive to. Feel prunes potential problems in the bud before they blossom into bombs. Feel is comfy in silence, no longer needing to fill the space. Feel is an intuitionalist, and a rationalist, and realist, and a minimalist, and is full of hope. Feel allows you to know something of the unknowable. Feel leads by following. Feel is the genius that teaches horse people how to listen to horses and people. We can practice this!

#61

And this is the thing, you're riding too much in your mind. You're playing this video in your head about how it's supposed to look, and you're not in your body. Every time you think you're supposed to be doing something, your horse offers resistance.

This is what I want you to really understand: don't be afraid to be at the beginning. If you're afraid to be at the beginning, you are not going to make it to the end. It's okay not to know what you don't know. What's not okay is feeling like you have to present half understood ideas to your horse, because then you create problems. Work in the space where you are. Master the simple stuff. There's a lot of profundity in being okay with where you are.

If you listen to me, I can turn you into a good rider. But, what I'm going to ask you to do is to really choose consciously your responses to what I'm saying. If you're always preparing for a rebuttal, and I can't finish a thought, you're not going to get it. The art of riding well lays in listening well. If you can't hear me, if you can't listen to me, there's no way you'll be able to learn to listen to your horse. And I don't want to come to our lessons having to prepare myself for a war of ideas with you. I will not do that.

Here is not where we learn to be seen; it's where we learn to see. I want you to trust what you feel and let your thoughts go. When you're thinking too much about what you're doing, and you're thinking about doing this, and you're thinking about doing that, your mare can't understand you. I just want you to feel what the walk feels like, and I want you to feel what your body feels like on the horse, and I want you to be okay with that. The only thing I want you to do right now is learn how to be honestly.

As you're going around, more and more of the shield is falling off you like shed skin. I can see it because your horse is calming down. You don't need a crystal ball if you can read body language. And so, whatever you feel like you have to protect yourself from, leave it out of the saddle, because then, your horse feels like she has to protect herself from you. Don't bring the rest of world to this work; it's not allowed. Wherever else in life that you're brilliant, and you are, it doesn't matter right now. Just. Ride. Your. Horse. Don't think about riding your horse; ride your horse.

Listen to the sound of her hooves touching the ground. Train your mind to quiet down. Is the footfall even? That's what I want you to listen for. Is your body moving in synch with the sound of her steps? I don't want you to force it. I want you to feel it. I want you to observe it. Give yourself to her. This is what I meant when I said, "You don't train horses to change for people. You teach people how to change." I don't want her to be anything other than herself. But, what I do want is for you to be completely hers.

The worst thing you can have is a horse that feels like it has to protect itself from you. Fight is what horses do when they're feeling overpowered. Schematic training methods built out of broken horses devolved into savages or slaves whose strengths have been conquered is an idea that's outlived its usefulness for me. There are no colonizers in my barn. If you're going to be a trainer of horses in the tradition of love and respect, and co-creation in life and art, you must learn to listen to what your mare is telling you about how what you're asking her to do is making her feel. If it feels forced, it's not correct. If she's shielded, it's not right. And until she stops feeling like that, we're not moving on. Her being willing to work for you is all there is. It's not about obedience, it's about understanding and peace. Horses only give you what you've offered them.

And so what is the goal of all of this work? The goal is for the horse to have a supple spine, and a supple mind, and an open body for as long as possible, no matter their job. This is the holy grail of happy, horse-centered horsehumanship.

#62

…and you see how it's not necessarily what you're doing, but the confidence you have in what you're doing that calms her down or revs her up. When you start experiencing those out-of-control thoughts, she starts exhibiting out-of-control behaviors.

I would rather breathe into those scary spaces, and try and train you how not to think anything at all, and to be neutral, and observant so that you can stay relaxed, than you thinking, "Oh God, this is where it gets fun. I don't want that."

It's not going to affect what aids you give; it affects the quality of your aids. Because if you're thinking you want her to do one thing in your mind, while at the same asking her to do another thing with your body, you're sending her a double-bind message and all she can give you is resistance.

This is where the breath becomes a really wonderful master, because when you breathe correctly, it refocuses your whole self. And you see how, now, she's in her body too.

Do you feel how you have something to sit on. I mean, she's filling your leg up, because she's not protecting her mouth from the hand by dropping her back.

And I apologize, again, because I don't feel like I was being clear with my request, and so I think that may be part of the reason you got frazzled. So, I apologize for that.

And now you're really beginning to understand how you can unteach yourself how to be afraid: if you keep living yesterday, it's going to fuck up your tomorrow. So says your horse.

Do you remember, how two weeks ago, you were worried about her going down to that end of the arena? And because you were thinking that things were gonna go to shit, they did. And now they're not, because you decided those thoughts weren't useful.

This is the task in training horses, and in life: you eliminate whatever doesn't evolve you. Whatever is not for your healthy growth: out. Because it only stays with your permission. And it's a whole lot better, how old are you: fifteen? It's a whole lot better that you learn this lesson at fifteen than at forty.

This is the truth: you give yourself permission to be free. When you give yourself that permission, the light that leads your way starts to shine from your own heart, because you have the courage to keep your heart open and trust life.

Because that horse, she walked into what you had opened for her.

When you feel what is possible, that's the light. Beautiful lesson. Very good.

#63

Softness is a physical state. Lightness is a mental state. A soft horse gives you only her body: this is submission. A light horse gives you her body and her mind: this is willingness. When you have have her head but not her hind legs, you have softness. That trot that you just ended, that was lightness. You want to ride her mind instead of her body.

And because your mind is under control, your body is relaxed, and you can allow yourself to feel what you feel— which is deep listening. The more you can get to that place of allowing the work to happen, the closer you are to the truth of the work.

You saw how when we started trotting, she locked her body against your hands because she thought you were going to try to get her soft. But, when her inside ear came back and you gave the inside rein, she said, "Oh, she heard the whisper. She hears me. I don't have to be angry. I don't have to be afraid of having my body taken away from me. It's because I get afraid of having my body taken away that I get upset when she's in the saddle, and I make my body hard so that I can hear her, but I'm not going to listen until she does."

Everything you're figuring out about your body only makes sense when you're riding feelingly, not when we're riding emotionally. When her back is up, there's a whole lot of shit that you just don't have to do. You can allow yourself to be balanced enough to help her find her balance ... and your thighs move, and your seat moves, and your ribs move and you're just there, because she's not trying to escape you making her soft. Do you see how a light horse changes the whole space energetically? There is joy flowing from her mane and tail. She's super chill right now. Beautiful.

Lightness is what connects life to itself, like the sun and the moon and the earth. Softness is horse+rider=2. Lightness is horse+rider=1. And that's the thing, once horses know that you know how to follow their minds, they don't have a problem giving you their bodies. But, if you go after their body first, they shut down. They learn that helplessness is survival.

#64

You're very capable of doing that, because you do it. That's all of the fight: you're capable. People think that I lie to them when I tell them that, but I see it.

I got a card from a student who is an instructor that said, "Sometimes I think you believe in me more than I believe in myself." That's my job.

I think that's the biggest challenge that I face with students if they stick around: they get afraid that I believe in them, and that I believe in them enough to teach them how to change, and they get scared of the change… and then fight me not to change.

#65

1)

Breathe as deeply as you can into the nose—that makes the inhalation a little bit slower—and allow the lungs to fill up slowly with air so that the body begins to relax. Then, let the breath out as slowly as possible, either through the nose or the mouth. And what's likely going to happen, is that as the tension starts to break up, you'll feel a dissemination of energy throughout the body. It'll be warm.

So, instead of trying to get rid of the headache, breathe into it. Breathe into the pain. And just keep following your horse. You're sitting a bit off to the left. Yeah yeah yeah. Good.

Good. Don't try and make anything happen. Just close the hands, and be in contact where you need to be in contact, and follow it. This is your weekly lesson in being, and not necessarily doing anything. Good, and let's go the other direction.

(It was so crazy, though. The guy pulls up in his truck yesterday, and I'm cutting my lawn, and I tell him that I'll got get him a check, and he goes, "Just tell Nahshon I'm here." He says, "And here, while you're there give him the receipt." I go, "This is weird, what's going on?" in my brain, you know. And I came back down and said, "I'm Nahshon." He goes, "Oh, when I pulled up and saw you cutting the lawn, I assumed you were the help like we have at our place." In that moment I just wanted to vomit. And I told him, "Just so you know, I own all of this." He was terribly embarrassed.

But, it was just a really, really strange feeling…)

Good. Where are you at? Good, keep going. We want to try to get it to where that pressure lessens on the temples. And where you're holding tension, where you feel yourself holding tension, not thinking you're holding tension… But, when you get out of your head and into your body, where you feel yourself holding tension, focus on that place.

Good. So, let's just keep using the breath to ease the stress so that you're not feeling your heartbeat in your head. That could almost be a poem!

Good. And you see and the pressure from the tension is starting to lessen, and the breath is going deeper, and you're not trying to force yourself to calm down, and your horse is starting to free up in his movement. That's how I know your stress is softening. In meditation, that's what you do, you use the breath to confront the discomfort instead of trying to run from it. You observe without acting by placing your attention on the distraction, the pain, the thought, the discomfort, but without identifying with it, which, in turn, teaches you how to find yourself recharging in peace. It's a weird and beautifully effective way of surviving humanhood.

There… try and feel the skin around you ears and along your face. Let it start to relax a little bit. The skin on the forehead… make sure your eyebrows are soft… Good, soften the armpits, open the heart… Yes, very good.

I'm totally convinced Mr. Grey is an Enlightened One returned. He understands a whole lot about life. He's just clear. He's clear enough to listen. That's my goal too, to just be clear enough to listen so well that you hear what's not said. He understands very clearly where you're at and what you need. He's not giving you any more to focus on than you just relaxing into yourself.

Good. Keep following the breath. Keep following the breath. Keep following the breath. And trust the horse will show you where you need to go and how to get there. Now, this is the thing, is that, you know, when we come, sometimes, to a place of relaxation, and we stop trying to force our mind to be quiet, and we just allow whatever happens to happen—especially in places where the body is coming out of tension—then what happens is that sometimes we start to see thoughts just fly by in our minds like we're sitting at a red light watching cars pass through the intersection. If that happens, nine times out of ten, it's going to be things that need your attention and want your attention, and your job is to just let them pass through... to step back and observe them in the moment.

This is how we create space in our heads, by not trying to corral the mind. If the mind wants to run, don't chase it. It's kind of like the horses in the field: if they don't want you to catch them, there's enough room to where you won't. It's just like that, and you see them galloping around in big dust clouds and trying to run after them is totally useless. And you realize that when you get emotionally attached to trying to catch horses running around in a space that's too big for you to even think about catching them, and it's something that you feel you have to achieve, and your body starts to get tight, and you vision starts to get very tunnel-like, instead of accepting, that if the situation is as safe as possible, maybe it's better to just watch the beauty of horses running.

Yes, there, his neck is starting to soften. Yes, and anything that you feel you have to do in your head, breathe into it and just let it pass. That's what this conversation is about, it's about not being emotionally attached to the body. The body will have its headaches. The body will be born, live, and die. The body is allowed to do what the body does, but the body is not you. You observe the body in its bodying. It's a very useful thing, when you can differentiate you having a headache, and your body having a headache. So, if the body has a headache, and you can detach yourself from the headache, and you can look at the body that you're in, with its headache, then you can begin to understand where the headache is coming from, which, in your case, is work-related stress due to poor boundaries.

When you begin to understand the wisdom of detachment, you begin to learn how to master the body. You push the body, but you also have to take care of the body. It's like a car, it needs its oil changed. My Dodge, it needs the opportunity to stretch its legs out on the highway to keep the engine healthy, you know. This is me inside of my truck, and this is you inside of your body. Now you're starting to find it.

Now, the challenge might come in that there may be some tension (You see the horse letting go of all that stress?) at the heart's center, it might start to clammer. If you feel the tightening of the sternum, right between the pectorals, breathe into that space. Wherever you feel tension along the length of the body, from your perineum to your scalp, if you feel any tension in any of those spaces, breathe into that space. And what will happen it that as you start to breathe into those spaces, you begin to unplug clogged-up energies. Yeah, there we go. (See how his hips just opened up, and the horse just lifted its back? Crazy, isn't it?) And you see how, as you begin to open up to life along the spinal column, your affect begins to calm and brighten? I think that's the beautify of this work—it's all empirical.

Open the ears. Open the ears. Open the ears. Let the tongue spread out across the roof of the mouth, let it blossom open. Good. You feel the pressure on the temples starting to soften? Yes, good.

I agree, riding a horse correctly is a side-effect of a person's soft energy, calmed mind, and relaxed body. I've never thought of it that way, but it feels true, yes. But, for me, the brilliance of it is that your horse's energy is softened and his mind calmed and his body relaxed. It's beautiful to see that because you're lighter, he's allowed you in as one of his well-informed interests.

There, soften the throat. Let the muscles along the esophagus relax; that comes from relaxing the the tongue in the mouth. To give the tongue more room, let it lay on the palate. Push it up and let it lay behind the front teeth onto the palate. Your windpipe softens because the muscles along the esophagus are opened up a little bit more, and your frontline starts to get longer. Good, as a result, your ischia follow the horse's back, but your hands follow the horse's neck. You're not trying to ride each part of the horse with every part of your body.

Now, what I want you to focus on is keeping your gaze

in-between the horse's ears just above the poll so that you can see where you're going and begin to understand where your horse's attention is. Good. Give your eyes to his mind. (This is how I'm going to make the headache go away. Watch this.) Wherever he looks, I want you to follow the direction of his head with your eyes. That's it. That's it.

Now, what I want you to do is think about something you would like him to do. A small circle, maybe. Put that, and only that, in your mind... Yes. Very good.

How's the headache? It's gone? Good. Good work.

2)

It's okay. Good. Now, walk in your body and in your mind. Good, now halt. Don't brace. Good job. You're turning into an Enlightened One, too. You're finding it. It's beautiful.

I did this to show you... because your mental and intellectual faculties are really powerful, but the emotional attachment to that power is what rules a lot of your world. So this is what happens when we can take the emotion out of the metal and intellectual fortitude, because the emotion is the individual: "I have a headache." But, when you can have the courage to see that you are not your body, then you can say, "This body has a headache, and there really is no "I." There's just everything else, which is nothing at all." So, if the "I," the individual, puts my attention and my conscious effort on something outside of the pain... because the only thing allowing the pain to be there is my focusing on the pain. And when you stop focusing on the pain, and you're aware of it, like you're aware of the cars passing on the road, but we're not standing at the door looking to see whether the driver is a man or a woman, then we begin to understand that everything that's happening outside of ourselves only happens to us to the extent that we allow it into our awareness. And how awareness then turns into attention, and how attention then turns into focus, and then how that focus then turns into the internalization of whatever is happening externally. It's taking these many different personas that we are and claim and that we inherit from the world, and allowing each of these horses to have their own stall.

Stillness-Spirit-Soul-Mind-Human-Son-Man-Teacher-Student-Friend-Queer-Gay-Black-American-Coloradan-Denverite-born nine months after arriving to the party with my dad and leaving with my mom... The farther down the line I go from the Stillness, the more the internalization of those stuck-point like beliefs. The more the internalization of those stuck-point like beliefs, the more the devotion to those titles takes a raccoon paw-like hold. And it's understanding that in those moments when the weight of these roles becomes too heavy to stand inside of, you can climb up the ladder rungs of consciousness to find rest and recover your power. Just like you did today. You Macro-ed. You left you and saw out of that part of yourself that just sees, and then your whole body opened up, and your horse's body opened up, and you touched that place in Consciousness where you were able to share headspace with your horse. And you began to feel how the riding position becomes easy to hold when you stop trying to hold the riding position. This stillness comes from the movement, and the movement comes from following the horse. But you can't follow the horse's body if you don't quiet your mind.

If you think, "I have to stay on the horse," then your reason for holding your position is to try and not fall off of the horse, in which case it becomes a weapon and not as a tool for communication. You're using the horse's body to protect your body from your own fears. And so, at all costs, the horse must give its body to you. This is how resistance is born. Instead of each of you using each other's bodies as a tool for communication, and understanding that beyond the body, you both share this common space that's deeper than the aids, and tack, and discipline, and all of this stuff. There's a shared internal space that you can connect him to, depending on how you approach him. Do you believe that you have the power to even try to talk to him in a way other than force, or insistent solicitation?

And if you do, then there's this place of knowingness that happens where whatever the situation, wherever I find my body, my identification with my body determines whether or not I'll be okay. Do you see what I mean?

Now your horse is asking you. Do you feel him? He's like, "What do you want from me?" This is the art of riding a horse. And when you come into the space of riding horses in this way, and life being hard is usually what brings us to the space within ourselves of riding horses in this way... of challenges that just don't seem fair, but that we must carry... and it's neither good nor bad. Rather, it's just an assignment to be completed, a lesson to be learned in order to grow you.

#66

I have an adorable little barefoot, fifteen-year-old, 14 hand, chalk-grey Arabian mare in my barn whom I call Fairy Tale because her qualities of sentience are pure magic to my mind and heart. She was born with her left foreleg shorter than the right, and had a surgery meant to permit more length to her deep digital flexor tendon when she was three months old. The procedure didn't work as planned for Fairy Tale, though. It left her with a keloid where the connective tissue had been cut, a prescribed eventual inevitability of arthritis in her left knee, and no added leg length.

During one of our occasional lessons last Fall, Fairy Tale began limping on the left front leg. I had her person dismount and work was discontinued until she was able to get an appointment with a joint specialist a month and half later. More and more I'm beginning to see that a life in love with horses is not a question to be asked but, rather, a mystery to be lived. Fairy Tale returned to the barn from the vet clinic with an inconclusive diagnosis, edema fluid drained from her knee, a cortisone shot, and a generic rehab schedule to be implemented after six weeks of stall rest.

For the nearly two years that I've known Fairy Tale, whether at work or rest, she has always bore more weight on her left shoulder by arching her nose and tail out to the right like a waning crescent moon. I am not a veterinarian, but I could see that, three months in, the rehab schedule targets weren't being reached with implementation as prescribed, and we weren't able able to garner much in the way of medical guidance. The swelling was staying down more, but her eyes weren't happy, she wasn't moving any better, her mind was not calm, and her person was beginning to really worry that this could be Fairy Tale's state of being for the rest of her life. So began the treasure hunt for the pot of gold on the other side of the rainbow.

I've been a practitioner of Iyengar's method asana for ten of the last twenty-three years I've practiced yoga. B.KS. Iyengar was a yoga master who used yoga poses to cure himself of tuberculosis as a child. He later went on to develop a gentle form of therapeutic yoga with props (blankets, bolsters, blocks, and straps) that he used to treat serious illness.

I'm able to find heaven in every step when I have the courage to allow horses to teach me how to help them heal. They have taught me to see the spaces where they are stuck in their body are the places where their person's heart is not open. Fairy Tale's person had to go away on business for three months during which time she was added to my training schedule full-time to see if I could help her get better. Using B.K.S. Iyengar's method of helping people as inspiration, I developed an individualized program for Fairy Tale that focused on correcting her alignment, building her strength and stamina, quieting her mind, resting between sessions, and daily turning out in the pasture with her friends.

Goat on the Mountain Top is an exercise in which the horse stretches its top line by walking its hind legs forward towards its stationary forelegs. I've used it to cure kissing spine. It was invented by Francois Baucher to help horses overcome their fear of collection. But, due to how the movement brings the front legs more under the body, I used it to stretch and start breaking up the scar tissue that had formed in Fairy Tale's left front leg after her ligament snip. To strengthen her core and cardio, I long reined her up and down the softly sloping hills behind my house. I used the pedestal work to sculpt a proper halt out of her broken body and to quiet her feet and mind. The result: most notably, Fairy Tale's ability to work long and low in a balanced, calm, rhythmic trot on the long lines and under saddle. The smooth roll of muscle from her poll to her shoulder is reshaping the arc of her neck vertebrae by way of hind legs actively stepping well under her body and a properly engaged backbone. All that to say she has her eye sparkle back! Also, the same vet came a few weeks ago to do Fairy Tale's annual check-up, exactly a year to the day of her diagnosis, and there's no more arthritis.

#67

You have such a beautiful relationship with your mare, and that makes things so much easier. The fact that you know how to hold that space for her to trust you means that you're fair, even if you aren't always right.

And the fact that she can tell you that you're not doing as good as you should be doing in the work, or you're not doing as well as she knows you can can do…

And the fact that she can do that and you listen to her and try to figure out, "Okay, where do I need to change?"—that's huge. It's your willingness to hear her that lets you know where she needs your help.

She's changed so much, just since I've known her.

You're so good. Are you such a good mare? I'm so proud of you. Yes, I am.

I'm proud of you two; this is beautiful work.

#68

That said, many traditions of equitation are blossomed out of the premise of subjugation and bullying to such an extent that the horse's ability to ask questions was bred out. When we do that, we lose the beauty, but if we have the courage to trust their intelligence, what do we get? We help anxious horses calm down because we understand that their behavior is them telling us that what we are asking them to do doesn't feel good. We get horses who help us learn how they learn.

The more people I can help find their own feel for their horses, the more horses I can help keep out of the killer's pen. One of the top reasons horses end up there is because they don't meet their rider's expectations.

Horses are precious enough for me not to bully them. Many methods that we have don't work. And they're making me create a new language for the horses that being bullied around doesn't work for. This language is built on people finding where their fears are and not hiding from them by learning to understand that if we trust the breath to get us through, we will survive and grow in the ways we want to and must.

If I am not able to find a language to help a horse-rider pair communicate in a more healthy way with each other, then I've failed as a teacher. Sometimes, I do. Language is powerful. Language is everything, and if I can bend it to my will, and use it to guide people to quiet their minds enough so that they can feel something…

Love reigns supreme here. For me, that's the value a true teacher holds: you believe in your students until your students believe in themselves to understand that people let the horse find answers when they trust feel. It's crazy that some of my students are old enough to be my parents and this is what I'm doing for them, and they trust me to do that. But, I've created a space in which we can all say, "I don't know what's happening right now" and be safe.

All of this goes back to my mom who taught me how to create a safe space to really feel and share what you feel. And what I'm really beginning to understand is that even though there are so many people in the world, we're alone with ourselves all of the time. When we're alone with ourselves all the time, our brains create problems, you know, and being able to understand that, and to honor that this is all of our process and then to teach people how to identify that process and disengage from it if we want, and to see that, then, exemplified by how horses answer the questions we ask them.

The horse spooked because the rider was worried about the cat, but the cat wasn't there. The rider was worried about the cat jumping out and spooking the horse, and so the horse spooked anyway. So I told the rider to make the space disappear, and it didn't happen again. So it's just teaching people how to use their minds in such a way that they're able to open the space up that they need to walk into.

When we're possible, when we know that we're possible, we create a vision for ourselves, and start walking the road to bring it to fruition.

She used to speak really badly about herself. She used to speak really badly about her horse. I told her, "If you can't stop, you can't stay here." The self-deprecation. It's in my contract: everybody respects everybody. We all respect each other: horses, cats, and people. If you can't do it, you've got to go. Love reigns supreme here. That's why the horses are quiet, because the energy is really lovely and peaceful. It's a whole world that we're all beginning to feel safe being inside of together.

Now she's starting to find the language. Did you hear that? When she said, "I'm wearing my week and I've spent the last hour trying to ground so that I could let the week go." She didn't used to have language for that. Then she would just expect her horse to come into the lesson and just deal with it, and of course her horse wouldn't respond correctly. She's understanding that when she can let that go, hearing the horse happens. It's beautiful. It's so beautiful.

And there are times when I'll come down here late at night and just cry. Just because of all the stuff going on in the world, and all of the pain in the world, and when you are sensitive like that, you feel it all. But, I'm beginning to understand that me taking care of myself in that way is what allows me to find the language to help my students find the language, so that they know themselves. That's a really scary thing to confront sometimes: to acknowledge that sometimes just leaving my farm is a scary thing, because the world is what it is, you know.

And understanding that, though it may be for different reasons, everyone has that button, everybody has that space, where just one more inch this way, and I'm beyond my capacity to feel anything because I've gone into fear mode. This is how almost all of my horses have arrived. And that issues that we're working through is them saying, "My fear muscles are exhausted, and I can't do this." And if we don't have that space where we can identify that within ourselves, there's no way we can help them, you know. There's no way that we can possibly hear them saying, "Everybody else I've worked with has hurt me." There's no way to understand that.

People have so much in their lives riding on being able to make life work for their horse. When it's not working, their taking that as a reflection of there effectiveness to be a whole human being. And they live, then, out of that space of 'I'm not as good as I want to be, and since I don't know how to be better, I have to accept not being happy with this situation. Then it begins to cloud their lens on the rest of the world, and they begin to present themselves to the rest of the world as "This is my problem and I have to live with it forever…" I think most true definition of help is when you find an answer better than the one you have, and how that's a constant, constant process of growth.

She just told me about how for the first six months of here time here, she would cry all the way to her lesson because she was just so afraid. But then working in that space… And there have been times when she would fidget, and she'd climb up on the mounting block, and she'd climb down and she'd move it, and she'd do it again, and that was all her way of stalling. I'd tell her, "Go for a walk, and don't come back until you're ready to try, because you're stuck. You're stuck in your head, and your horse is feeling it. Leave it alone, and come back to the mounting block when you're ready." And because we honored that space, now she is able to just come in and hop right on. So, instead of allowing her to stay stuck in this cycle of fear she had no language for, I'd have her walk her horse around the arena until she could find calm and was ready to try again. Now, a year later, she comes in to the arena and says, "This is the stress I had from the week, and this is what I've done to address it, and now I'm getting on."

I don't believe in shoulds because I don't have to win. This is not about winning. It's not about winning. It's not about either of us winning or losing. Winning and losing has everything to do with "doing." I don't do that anymore. I've won a lot of stuff in that world, and I've gotten a lot of recognition for that, the world over. But, my horses weren't happy.

People need information presented to them in ways they understand best. And there just aren't a lot of really effective ways to teach people how to connect with their horse. They watch great riders ride, but then they don't know what the great riders are doing. Then you have great riders trying to explain with they're doing, but they can't. And then feel becomes this mysterious thing endowed to a chosen few by the gods of horsemanship because there is no language for it. But, when we can put language to it, we can get really magnificent stuff from our students. And that is hugely empowering!

Full disclosure: I don't understand life with horses as a

metaphor. They are the filter. They are my bridge from the known to the unknown and a safe way back for me.

I vote for people by asking, "If I were a horse, would I want them to be my trainer? Do they have that kind of compassion and empathy to listen? Do I trust how this person is making me feel when things aren't good?" That's an omen. Horses are teaching me how to go through life. We're sharing this space together, right now, because I trust them. That means the world to me.

If I can help other people that by teaching them how to ride correctly, because that's really what's happening… teach them how to deal with stress effectively so that they can let it go… This is fucking amazing. Everybody has that ability.

I just want to say, I appreciate you being open to having this conversation with me. You stayed. That tells me the type of person you are. Horses taught me to trust that. And I really appreciate you being interested in my process of working with my students and my teachers. It means a lot that you have access to the work of some many great people of the horse, and that you're reading this, now, and are interested in what I might have to offer to the conversation.

And my goal is to be great. I want to be one of the best of my generation, and I will know that I'm earning my seat when I can help people understand that being afraid is a learned behavior, which means that it can be unlearned, so that we can move on with the work. And this is my process for riding students:

1) We aren't ashamed that we're afraid.

2)   We begin to explore and understand what "it" is we're afraid of.

3)   We begin to explore and understand how we learned to be afraid of "it."

4)   What value does being afraid of "it" hold?

5)   How does being afraid of "it" help you?

6)   If "it" doesn't help you, do you want to choose to hang on to being afraid of "it?"

7)   Oh, I understand. You don't have a substitute behavior.

8)   Let's create a substitute behavior.

9)   That's what we're asking our horses to do: to feel safe enough to be willing and try to learn a better way to be in the world, even when, sometimes, it doesn't feel like it's worth the effort.

That's it. That's the whole process. Language. That's what pushes me to keep studying.

Sometimes, it feels like there's a hesitancy toward science from people who believe that it diminishes the horse's mystery...or being-ness. They're afraid to think about anatomy and neuroscience in their practice of horsehumanship. I think that's an excuse for willful ignorance. And I challenge that by saying, "What you're doing isn't working. Are you open to the possibility of another answer?" That's what Ray Hunt was doing, even if he didn't know he was doing it. And this is what makes it possible for you to do what Ray Hunt was doing.

Now, was Ray Hunt a genius? Absolutely. Nuno Oliveira? Yes! The Dorrance brothers, were they geniuses? Yes! Almost to the point of being avatars. They had an understanding of horses that was so beyond what so many people had experienced. I think more people should be able to do that.

"I see that when I do this, it makes my horse uncomfortable." That comes from cultivating a place of openness and non-judgement and respect for the horse's sentience. That's feel. And you can't have feel unless you know how to relax. Correct riding is about listening to horses. Period. When we do that, classical horsemanship is natural and natural horsemanship is classical.

We all must feel safe enough to be real with each other; this is the key to working well with horses: that communication is clear enough to the point of there not being any maybes. When there are, everyone is confused and masking it behind politeness and hope, or force. There's no place for that to get things done. Nobody's dignity has to be compromised.

I don't look at the art of training horses as a religion. It's not this doctrine that's unquestioned or unquestionable. There's no need for worship. It is a living thing. It's a friendship. It's a love affair. We grow. We fuck up, we apologize, and we move on. That's it.

It is sacred. And for it to be real, it needs to be questioned. There is an air of reverence here, though. Meaning that when the arena becomes a work space of experiential praise, the joy is in the horse trying to do what I'm asking it to do with its body.

True horsemanship is not the worship of these great people outside of ourselves but, rather, each of us finding that space inside of ourselves, as best we can, and working from it. That's all the masters did.

My work is not about me; it's about the horses. It's about unveiling what is possible when we have a bridge to cross. It is understanding that my work as a teacher is being down on my knees and building every brick for my students to take each step across the canyon. That's my work.

#69

And Nova was like, "Look, I promised that if you had the courage to take care of me, I'd take care of you. I've gotten you here. Now we need to stop and recalibrate and see what things are." When horses do that, for me, I'm usually able to initiate a conversation with them to see what is going on. But with him, I was just met with silence. He wasn't upset, and he was still super-social and engaging and his beautiful cuddly self, but there was just this semi-colon. We really needed to take a little bit of a pause.

He really likes doing trick training. Nova loves trick training, so we did some pedestal work for a while, and went for strolls around the farm, and his body started to relax and open up again. Then, last week I went into the arena, and I just didn't know what to do. So, we did some work on his pedestal, and then I sat down, and I just... I just started to cry because I didn't know what he wanted me to do. And for an hour, while I wept, he stood over me, and rested his chin between my shoulder blades, and just breathed into my body, and said, "I know all the movements. Now, let's see how much softer into these movements we can go. You're in a new world; now you have to learn how to be in it, and I'll teach you."

When I don't have the answer, I just wait. I just wait. I quiet myself down...and waiting is scary...

I try to be effective. And I try to set intentions that are healthy and beautiful and worthy of life. But, when my best horse so far says "We need to re-correct a little bit"…me as a person, I can act like I didn't hear him and barge though. Or, I can respect what he says. The thing about that horse, that he has taught me, is that horses are never wrong.

I like horses with trauma helping me understand the intention behind the questions that they hear me asking, so that they can teach me how to work out of a deeper inner-space of unpolluted clarity, which then, in turn, helps them trust me enough to relax. My effectiveness with these horses resides in me having no agenda or plan to follow, and just letting them show me where they want to start, and allowing them to lead me through that, which, in turn, has taught me how to listen deeply.

#70

In my dreams
Nova blesses the air

As he carries my hopes
Heavenward

With galloping hooves
Sounding off

Like prayer flags
Snapping in the wind

His body
Is my soul

He is the breath
My mind rides

Like an escaramuza
Astride her best mount

Creating karma
With thought

#71

Our anger is a result of what we are afraid of. Anger is an indicator of fear. If the horse isn't doing what this kiddo wants, the kiddo is afraid of losing control of the horse. So the kiddo punishes the horse.

With the students I work with who are struggling with anger issues, what I have found, is if it's something I'm asking them that they get angry at, it's usually because they don't understand what I'm asking, and I really have to ask them: "How do you want me to communicate with you? How do you learn?" In doing that, you're teaching this child how to express what they need.

Your job as a teacher of students who hang with you for a while is to teach teachers.

So, if you see this kiddo struggling, it's because they don't feel heard. Angry people don't feel heard, and that's what they're afraid of.

If this kiddo has a blowout with their horse, I think it's important to pause and explore with them what they were asking: How did you ask? And if the horse didn't do what you wanted done, what's a way we could ask that differently?" Also worthy of exploration with this young one is what kind of relationship do they want with their horse?

Do you want a horse who feels like a slave who can't answer questions? Or, do you want a horse who is a friend you can trust? Horses who are trained out of fear, you can't trust them.

So, I think that from a teacher point-of-view, really having a deep conversation, as deep as you both feel comfortable having, about "How can I help you with this anger. Because I see that when it hits, you're in a really unhappy space on your horse, and I know how much joy horses bring you. And I just want to help you keep that joyful space through the difficult situation you may be having with your horse." I think that may be a really helpful way to confront that. It's really true, and it's really honest, and it's supportive, and you're expressing your concern in a way that's respectful. Language is everything.

But what is sounds like, for some reason, is this kiddo is super stressed out. Maybe their parents are too hard on them, or they're too hard on themselves. But, I think if you have that relationship with them, it's important to have a conversation around that too, like: "What's making you feel like this?" "How can I use language to check in with you before you get on to make sure you're in a healthy space for your horse?"

Those are things that I do. Then, once they process their frustrations, they begin unearthing root causes for the emotions that they're expressing in an unhelpful way. It's exactly the same thing with horses. Horses are humans with different brains.

#72

This all blossoms out of a space where you're giving yourself the tools to support your students. Find how you're best comfortable in yourself doing that. When you have students who you love, it's really hard not to take them home with you. Find ways to let the day be done so you can rest and take care of yourself.

You can't give your students more than you give yourself. As their teacher, you're showing them how to achieve their goals, dreams, and hopes. But if you're not walking the path yourself, there's no way you can be the light for the person walking behind you.

In the end, it's all one thing. Your student under your tutelage, the people under your love, are only as possible as you create space for them to be possible, and to do that you have to create space for yourself.

It all stems from you. You are the root. Root systems don't grow without healthy soil, water, rest, and worms. It's important for your students to know that there's a boundary for them in your world so that you can take care of yourself.

It's a struggle for teachers. But, it's important that you find something that doesn't allow you to move that boundary up again. People will always allow you to run yourself into the ground for them.

I think true riding teachers are the holders of a holy and wonderful tradition of being human and we have to take care of ourselves. Super important.

As you begin to manage your life and take care of yourself, you're able to suggest helpful ways for your students to do the same. I talk about it all the time with my long-term students. The ones who don't change their lives, usually don't deem it worth the trouble to continue studying with me. That's OK with me.

When people's lessons start improving, usually so too do their lives. If you're guiding them through that, you have to do it for yourself first. It's very important you not sacrifice yourself. It's hard, I know.

That's why you're reading this, because I set time aside every night to write. Writing the meditations about my horses and students is how I let them go—for the night. Take care of yourself.

My step-dad, before he died, told me, "You first." The most unselfish thing you can do is to take care of yourself so you're there for your students, and everyone else in your life.

It's important that you give them something that they enjoy receiving from you, and that you enjoy giving to them, and they give those parts of themselves to you, and then everyone is happier. Then you begin to recognize the folks who aren't healthy for you and find the courage to remove yourself from the situation as respectfully as possible.

I don't even know what question I'm answering, but it's just really important because at the heart of all of your questions comes back to you taking care of yourself so that you have space to rest, so you can offer them the space to learn how to rest.

Horses are lovely, and I think it behooves us to take care

of ourselves so we can have them around as long as possible. No, I'm serious. There are consequences for not taking care of ourselves. It's important that you love yourself as well as you love your most-loved horse.

It's important that you find the value in knowing what makes you healthy, and doing that. And the people who have a hard time taking care of themselves really struggle with feeling like they deserve to do that. But, nobody's going to give you permission to take care of yourself but you.

That's where your boundaries grow out of. That's where your relationships grow out of. That's where everything grows out of: what you feel you're worthy of having.

This is where horses lead us into some really deep heart work, some really deep emotional work, some really deep work around self-worth, and value, and all of this stuff. It's really easy to get lost in loving then so much that we use that as an excuse to not take care of ourselves. That's just not okay.

And the reason, as a teacher, that's not okay, is because that's what you're teaching. This is the heart of growth. Self-care, or a lack there-of, is a really bad problem among professionals in the horse world.

This is how we burn out: we get to places where we feel like we can't have anything wrong in our world because we present ourselves as this altruistic savior for the people in our realm. That's unfair, and it's total bullshit.

You must take care of yourself. It's really, really important. Then your horses will start doing better, too. Horses respond to energy, first. And if a horse isn't sure about what you want them to do, it's because the horse isn't sure about what you're asking them to do, and that just might be because you're too emotionally, physically, or mentally tired to be clear. Healthy, un-broken spirited horses are embodiments of their people's minds.

You look at videos of Nuno Oliveira on his horses, and you see the focus on his face. He was in another world. He looks almost like a statue on these horses, because he was so focused, and his horses felt safe because that's what he was for them.

That's just it: you know the people who are healthy for you by the one's who support you doing things that are healthy for yourself. It makes everything else a lot easier when you see how people support how you love yourself.

And we were talking about feel, understanding the intention behind your question. By listening to the questions you asked, this is what the heart of my answer to you is: you have to take care of yourself.

When you can listen to the intention behind a question, you start hearing horses. I just did with you what I do with horses. This is speaking, but this is truly what they're saying. It's magic. And this is how you're possible, right? You are the light. You're only as possible as you are able to see the light. Possibility is the light. The sun and the moon. It's not some mystic thing.

From that place, healthy boundaries are born. From that place, healthy horses are built, and broken horses are pieced back together again and healed—people, too. Does that make sense?

#73

I once heard it said

If a feeling of gratitude arises
because you see
that you are living
in answered prayers
or underserved grace
then it is beautiful
and you find peace

I've found peace
Horses are peace

#74

1)

When I'm working with horses, it's not in time. That is not where I'm at. I'm on earth, but am in another place where my devotion to the small and seemingly insignificant process of understanding a deeper horse-human connection is only limited by my unwillingness to be honest and open with myself.

2)

And this is my work: to forget what I've learned enough to find my self on the inside of myself before reaching out to express my heart's humble hope for a horse to help me help them. Then, if they feel safe, the horse will offer to share its spirit with me to show me where to go to find the question to the answer.